Mistake-Proofing Leadership

Second Edition

Mistake-Proofing Leadership

Second Edition

Rudy F. Williams, Ph.D.   Robert A. Brown, Ph.D.

bp books

© 2019 Robert A. Brown

All rights reserved

Printed in the United States of America

Requests for permission to use or reproduce material from this book should be directed to books@collwisdom.com

Published by bp books
11700 Mukilteo Speedway 201, PMB 1084
Mukilteo WA 98275
USA

Library of Congress Control Number: 2018964729

ISBN-13: 978-0-9998667-3-3

To all those who are making
the world a better place and to the
memory of my friend, Rudy Williams.

INTRODUCTION

Soon after the publication of the first edition, the authors were fired from their internal consulting jobs in an event we called "The Pill Hill Ambush and Massacre." In separate meetings on a Monday morning, our boss presented this logical progression:

1. You wrote a book
2. You did not ask permission
3. Not asking permission showed poor judgment
4. If you have poor judgment, I can't trust you
5. If I can't trust you, you have to be fired

Of course, we were not fired because we wrote this book. The book was written on our time, on our computers and said nothing negative about anyone. We believe we were fired because we wrote the truth on our boss's performance review, foolhardy perhaps, but we wanted to be loyal to our organization. Yet, like so many before us, we found ourselves marching out the building carrying our belongings in a cardboard box. That was certainly a real-life lesson about values, and we would do it again.

Over the following weeks, we meet at a train station halfway between our homes for coffee and hot chocolate and to adjust to our new situation and discuss what to do next. It took a while, but we later enjoyed the delicious irony of losing our jobs because of an inadequate leader for ostensibly writing a book about improving leadership.

We also discussed what could have been different at work. Should we have somehow influenced our boss or met privately with our bosses' boss to address our concerns?

To us, our boss was not competent, did not have the skills or character needed for the job. However, we feared any dialogue would not be a two-way street. We did not trust our boss and took the easy route of saying so on the performance review.

The ambush and massacre put a visceral spin on our understanding of poor leadership and the dynamic of mistrust. It highlighted the power inherent in leaders who must control, be right, and who dismiss differing opinions. Such leaders create a power base demonstrating the difficulty of opposing this kind of power. It also highlighted the value of creating trust, teams, mutual visions and open communication.

Our train station meetings became an opportunity to reflect on our actions and our next moves (both then being in our mid 60s). We decided to individually find new positions, continue to support one another and our mutual efforts to improve leaders. We did so with renewed energy. Significant changes were needed in how organizations are run.

Our experience documents the damage that can be caused by a flawed leader and renewed our passion for books like this one; helping regular people become true leaders. We use business as our platform, but anyone who leads or aspires to lead others will benefit from the ideas and concepts we present.

Sadly, most managers and leaders are undertrained and under-supported. Happily, they are not bad leaders, only not yet up to the task. Many of them were skillful at their jobs and were then promoted into positions where they must survive by intelligence, personality, shooting-from-the-hip, what worked before and what others tell them to do. The result is increased stress in everyone, lower morale, and eventually breakdowns in personnel and productivity.

However, there is a solution. Learn how to mistake-proof your leadership. This book on mistake-proofing leadership will teach you how to harness the wisdom of employees and enable you to know what to do, when, and how.

Benefits of mistake-proofing:

1. Leaders are leading emotionally engaged employees
2. Best solutions are assembled by people working together; not by simply reaching consensus
3. All employees are on high-performing teams
4. Employees take ownership of processes, improve them, and increase capacity

Much has changed in the ten years since we first wrote *Mistake Proofing Leadership*, some of it has been what Rudy and Bob have additionally learned about supporting leaders and those they lead.

Our approach uses storytelling, drama, struggle and triumph to help readers see and feel the power of concepts that go beyond anything currently available in leadership development.

Our intention is that you will change your current leadership in many ways, in what you know how to do, what you consider important to your leadership, and how you will enhance those you lead. Specifically, we hope you will:

- Want to become a true leader rather than remain a leader in name only
- Have a greater appreciation for and accountability to those who follow you

- Unleash the leadership of those you lead
- Use bundles of appropriate behaviors to mistake-proof your leadership

Mistake Proofing Leadership has been inspired by true leaders, great teachers and insightful colleagues as well as driven by personally encountering too many mediocre leaders. Yet, we are optimistic about the world and honor leaders who solve problems currently thought to be too difficult, support others and act with a strong moral compass.

We encourage leaders in any endeavor to apply the lessons of this book and thereby join us in our quest to improve the world. Our intent is that your employees are better for having worked with you.

We hope you find yourself in our story and become one of the heroes.

* * *

Rudy and Bob discussed updating the book over the past few years, but unfortunately did not complete the work before Rudy became ill. The task then became a labor of love and honor for Bob to complete.

We've updated some of the concepts, explained them better and polished the prose here and there. We hope this second edition further educates readers of the initial book and inspires those reading it for the first time. There is leadership to be improved and a world to take care of. We'll give you good ideas of how to do that.

CONTENTS

PART I THE COLLABORATIVE

1   THE INVITATION 1
2   THE INTENSIVE 9
3   THE FOUR PILLARS 37
4   PONDERING 58
5   THE ZEN OF LEADERSHIP 64
6   BUILDING TEAMS 73
7   A TEAM WITH A VISION 87
8   HARNESSING THE SPEED OF THOUGHT 99
9   DELEGATING 110
10 CUSTOMER AND EMPLOYEE LOYALTY 118
11 INTRODUCING A CHANGE 130
12 ORGANIZATIONAL CHANGE 138
13 TIME 147
14 COMMUNICATING 153
15 LEARNING ORGANIZATIONS 158
16 MISTAKE-PROOFING MISTAKE-PROOFING 165
17 ROSE 183
18 A CALL TO ACTION 195

PART II REFLECTIONS

REFLECTIONS 201
1. THE INVITATION 203
2. THE INTENSIVE 204
3. THE FOUR PILLARS 205
4. PONDERING 208
5. THE ZEN OF LEADERSHIP 209
6. BUILDING TEAMS 210
7. A TEAM WITH A VISION 211
8. HARNESSING THE SPEED OF THOUGHT 212
9. DELEGATING 213
10. CUSTOMER AND EMPLOYEE LOYALTY 214
11. INTRODUCING A CHANGE 216
12. ORGANIZATIONAL CHANGE 218
13. TIME 219
14. COMMUNICATING 220
15. LEARNING ORGANIZATIONS 221
16. MISTAKE-PROOFING MISTAKE-PROOFING 222
17. ROSE 223

INDEX 225
THE AUTHORS 229

Part I

THE COLLABORATIVE

1

THE INVITATION

I ripped open the envelope. The letter inside was more important to me than the one from Berkeley or the one from Michigan. I was younger in those days, eager to learn, ripe for new experiences. Now, older and accomplished, I should have been calm, more dignified, but I wasn't. I was as excited as a new dad and almost as scared. This was a huge opportunity and one that also included the prospect of revisiting past mistakes, some of which still make me wince.

The first words said it all, "We're delighted to offer you a space in the next Mistake-Proofing Leadership Collaborative."

I'm the CEO of Rowdell Software, a company that customizes software for small and medium-sized businesses. We're making money, growing at a good rate, have low employee turnover, and I'd like to keep it that way. A friend of mine, Hal, who owns a half dozen furniture stores, told me about something called Collective Wisdom, Inc. I thought it was similar to other groups such as The Executive Committee and I told him, "No, thanks." The idea of businesspeople getting together with a facilitator to talk business is okay with me; it just doesn't mesh with my idea of practicality. I find most such conversations useful for about half an hour and seminars good for maybe an hour. By then things get repeated or off track and I get antsy. At the same time, I know some people who are geniuses whose brains I'd love to pick. My experience has taught me a lot, but there is much more to learn. If somehow only the most helpful or important material was covered, I'd go much more often than I do, but that rarely happens.

Hal said, "Wait a minute, don't go saying 'no' before you know what you're saying 'no' to."

"Okay," I said. "I'm listening."

"Here's the deal. Collective Wisdom is two guys with a great idea." Hal paused, seemingly for dramatic effect and pointed his index finger at me. "The idea is that businesses are run by smart people who have learned a lot in school and on the job, yet these smart, experienced people still make monumental mistakes. Right?"

"I'm proof of that," I agreed.

"Then you should ask yourself, how come? Why do you make mistakes? Why does anyone make a mistake?"

"You're asking me why people make mistakes?"

"Yeah."

"Hal, it sounds suspiciously like you're beginning to make a sales pitch, but I'll bite. People, even the best business leaders, are human and humans make mistakes. Is that the answer you're looking for?"

"Yes. Now think of your doctor. Say you have to go in for delicate surgery. Would you be okay if your doctor was only human and made a mistake? Of course not! Your surgeon making a mistake would be unexpected and terrible."

"Okay."

"So what these two guys do is apply to business what works in medicine. And apply what works in some businesses to all businesses."

"Keep going."

"The approach used when your surgeon cuts into you is called 'best practices.' This 'evidence-based medicine' is the gold standard, what research has shown is the best method currently known based on clinical evidence. They record everything they do, share results and constantly improve their techniques. Now, let's say you have a heart attack."

"This sure is a fun discussion."

As usual, Hal ignored me and continued without pause. "If you had a heart attack, your doctor would treat you with what they call a treatment 'bundle' which are all those things known to improve an outcome. You have a heart attack; they know the six things that are supposed to be the absolute best treatment. If they do only five of the six you don't get as good a result. The two guys I'm talking about teach leadership bundles."

"Intriguing."

"There's more."

"Keep going."

"You know about the success of the Toyota Manufacturing System, where they've worked for 50 years to eliminate all types of waste. They also work toward perfecting their production processes by using what they call poka yoke, self-check and successive check."

"I know about Toyota and Lean Thinking. I like the approach."

"Well, these guys have expanded the idea from something called Lean Thinking 4.0 and applied it to leadership. It's the best thinking from Toyota applied to people interactions. You can't get better than that. I took their Mistake-Proofing Leadership collaborative. It was fantastic. It was all about how I could mistake-proof what I do every day."

"So now you're perfect?"

Hal smiled. "A whole lot closer than I was before I took the workshop. And I want you to take it. You need to experience how solid the material is and how well it works."

"I don't know. Taking a class…how long is it?"

"Twelve weeks. Two hours a time. And it's definitely not just a class; it's a collaborative workshop."

I held up my hand to stop the discussion. "Not for me. That's almost an entire semester. Been there and done that. I'd get more out of a book in one fourth the time – on my own schedule, too, and for a lot less money. And I could enjoy a cup of coffee by the fire while I was reading."

"There's also a six-hour intensive meeting before the weekly meetings and pre-work before you even get started."

"Well, that sells the idea even more. Listen, Hal, it may have been useful for you, but in truth, you're younger and less experienced than I am. I've had more classes than I care to remember. Some were good, some were great, and some were a total waste of time. Since then I've learned on the job, which is probably the best way. I admit I've made some mistakes, but not too many and not overly bad ones. The business is going well. My wife loves me. The kids are doing great in college. I just bought a new driver that gets me 30 more yards down the fairway. I'm a happy man."

"So why learn anything more? Is that what you mean?"

"I'm not saying that. I'm always open to learning. I just don't want to waste my time."

"Exactly. The collaborative doesn't waste time. You learn a skill, try it out, report on it the next week and problem solve with other bright, experienced people. They say 30% of the time is being introduced to new material and 70% of the time you solidify your learning by applying it in your work. The idea is that you do leadership activities anyway, but now you'll do them in a new and better way."

I groaned, but Hal pressed on. "Let's say you want to introduce a change, like moving everyone who is hourly to salary. You can imagine how many different points of view there would be about that.

"From the collaborative experience, you learn the best way to do it, you try it out, you report on how it went, the other participants give you feedback, and you learn how to do it even better. Then you learn a new skill and the cycle repeats. By the end, you've done a lot of new things that improved both you and the business."

That seemed like a nice idea. "Are you getting a commission from these guys?"

"I just think they're great. The concept is good, the topics are right, they present the material well, and it works. You can't beat that."

"Okay, these guys are great, and the workshop is wonderful. Exactly how have you changed?"

"Good question. Before this collaborative, I pretty much stuck with what worked in the past. My leadership was based mostly on my personality, some on figuring things out on the fly, and some on just taking my best guess about what might work. Today I have models to apply to most situations. I know which model to use and how to use it. I know what results to expect. I even have ways to know immediately if what I'm trying to do is the right thing to do. My confidence has soared because I don't have to guess; I have skills. And what's even better, I share my skills with all my employees. They have learned how to help me do my job of helping them. It's almost scary how effective knowing and applying the right model is. Everyone wins."

"Okay, I'll consider it," I told him, and then changed the subject. We were walking to the 14th green and I wanted to get away from thinking about work while I had a chance to birdie the hole.

* * *

I was good to my word and did consider it. I've always believed a great leader is someone who unleashes the leadership potential in those around him and I wanted to be a great leader. I wasn't a great leader then, so Hal's suggestion was intriguing.

I called Collective Wisdom and talked with Rudy, one of the two guys Hal mentioned. They offered several different programs, but the one Hal took sounded like the best for me. I quickly decided I wanted to join the next collaborative and naturally Rudy said the next one was full; they accept no more than eight participants. Like most people, when I can't have something, I want it more. He told me the next Mistake-Proofing Leadership

Collaborative would begin in two months, but I didn't want to wait. I had to get in now.

That's why I was so excited to get the letter. What made me anxious was another thing Rudy said, "Participants are required to show up on time, participate fully, listen intently, tell the truth, trust the process and honor commitments." It's their basic agreement and it made sense. I have no problem listening and I can tell the truth as well as the next person, but I don't relish the idea of critiquing myself in front of others if some of my less successful efforts come up for discussion. Some, like the firing of one of my managers, were recent and didn't go well. I was probably most worried about any blind spots I might have, where I think I know what I'm doing when I really don't. It isn't easy taking an in-depth look at yourself when you have a bit of ego invested in what you already know.

But I was in. I wanted to stretch and learn. I wanted the best for me, the best for my business and the best for my employees. I immediately put the six-hour intensive session on my calendar and soon enough the day to play arrived.

2

THE INTENSIVE

Ten of us (eight participants and our two facilitators) sat around the table chatting. We planned to be together for the next six hours. At exactly eight-thirty, Bob stood up and started the collaborative with a bang.

"Good morning, everyone. I'm Bob. True leadership is obvious, compelling and unifying. It is rare. Nominal leadership is divisive, short-sighted, uninspired, wasteful, collusive and disruptive. I could go on. Unfortunately, nominal leadership is all around us. I have known only one true leader in my life. I want to tell you about him. He is also a 'Bob.'

"Bob Carrie was a child psychiatrist I met just a couple of years out of psychology graduate school. I was filled with wonderful theories and I was intent on revolutionizing mental health care. The first stop on my change-the-world tour was at a publicly funded guidance clinic near the California-Mexico border. Our patients were mostly low-income families who paid either nothing or were on a low sliding-fee scale. Every Tuesday, Dr. Carrie arrived at the clinic with a box of donuts to spend an hour consulting with each of six child/adolescent service providers.

"He was probably in his sixties, mid-size, beginning to bald and entered rooms with a warm smile and a warmer handshake. He had been a Marcus Welby type family doctor in Michigan before taking advanced training in child psychiatry. It was his job to help us fully understand our patients and provide the care they needed.

"I didn't know anything about leadership in those days. Didn't know much about anything really. You could probably best describe me as enthusiastic and optimistic. During our hour together Bob and I talked about everything, beginning with the cases I presented. Early on that's all we talked about. But as my skills grew, we discussed bigger ideas, like my contribution to the development of the child/adolescent service, and later my budding leadership of the clinic itself. He would carefully listen to my observations of patient or clinic problems, ask leading questions, solicit my opinion as to what should be done, test my understanding of the entire process and wish me well. I was the center of that hour.

"He ran meetings with the same grace and effect. We all had a part in identifying problems and seeking solutions. I wouldn't say he was directing our meetings, but afterward I could see how he orchestrated our working together. There was debate, but always toward a group goal, never to win a debate point.

"When I compare his leadership to all others I experienced in the last thirty-some years, what stands out is his genuine appreciation of all the members of his team and the need each of us felt to never let him down, each other down, or our patients down. There was an irresistible pull toward doing what was right."

Bob stopped his story and looked at each of us in turn. "Our goal is for each of you to become a true leader, someone like Bob Carrie who still leads me thirty years after our last hour together." He sat down and Rudy stood up.

"I also have a story of a true leader. My example is relatively recent, within the last few years. Melody Cartwright was a director to whom I reported in a large corporation. She was charged with developing executives and other formal leaders and had daily contact with the executive team. I admire Melody for many reasons. She was a superb listener who easily grasped abstract concepts, including my own emerging ideas. She quickly unearthed gems in even my most outrageous propositions and routinely integrated them with her own thinking. Her frequent refrain, "Try it; learn from it" encouraged me and my colleagues to test our ideas, learn from them and test them again. It also demonstrated her trust in us and her comfort with ambiguity. She balanced this risk-taking with a pragmatism that demanded a quick, though not horrific, pace. Things got done with Melody at the helm.

"As an unwavering advocate of customers, she focused on those whom she served: end-use customers, leaders, staff, me. We who reported to her were the beneficiary of her belief that working with and through people required that she develop them. She repeatedly supported my growth by encouraging me to pursue my interests and by opening doors for me throughout the organization. Her door, her mind and her heart were always open, and that made all the difference.

"Melody was a true leader for many others. A visionary searching for and finding possibilities extending far beyond current practice. I'm pleased to say that unlike leaders who receive little attention or acknowledgment, Melody received our corporation's highest leadership award, given to only one recipient each year."

Rudy paused for a moment, apparently lost in thought, and then said, "She left our organization to do important national work. I miss working together. We always focused on the well-being of our people and the success of our company."

Rudy slowly sat down.

If they wanted me to be inspired, those stories worked.

From his seat, Bob pointed to a flip chart labeled "OBJECTIVES." "These," he said, "are our objectives for today." As you can see, it was pretty simple.

> **OBJECTIVES**
> - Know what a nominal leader is
> - Know what a true leader is
> - Know what you must do to become a true leader

Although I didn't know the definitions they were using, I figured I knew of just a couple of true leaders and a barrel full of what they were calling nominal ones. The collaborative agenda called for participants to introduce ourselves and tell of our own experience with either a true leader or a nominal one, probably wanting to check out our assumptions about leaders. I asked to start us off. I told them my name and that I was CEO of Rowdell Software and was pleased that a few nodded their heads in recognition. My story had to do with my most recent boss, the one that had given me the courage to start my own company.

"While thinking about our assignment to bring a story of a great leader, a true leader, I realized that I had been assuming that most of my bosses had been if not great leaders at least good ones and was a bit shocked when I reflected back on all their flaws. Not that I expect anyone to be perfect. I've had maybe fifteen bosses in my career, and like Bob, I guess I had only one I would call a true leader.

"This was about fourteen, maybe fifteen years ago. I was middle management in the production department of Andrews Metals, a supplier for Boeing. The president was Larry Chapman, been with the company probably twenty years and had seen it all. My boss reported to him, and I had a fair amount of contact with him, too.

"What I remember most was the respect that people gave him. He wasn't authoritarian or formal, just the opposite. But when he walked into a room or even down a hall, you could tell he was the boss. He wasn't arrogant; you could just feel the confidence.

"The other thing was he had a vision for the company. He always said that if Boeing was going to be the global aerospace leader, they won't be able to do it without us. We were to partner with the biggest and the best. That meant we had to be the best, too. It would have been a disaster for us if Boeing chose another supplier, so we made sure everything we did was better than anyone else. We knew we were good and worked hard to prove it every day. It was like everything was possible if we followed Larry Chapman."

Rose Murray, on my left, went next and told us about her company president. She was followed by Sid Whitman. He talked about a little league baseball coach. Fourth to go, John Tiles chose to talk about a nominal leader, a leader in name only, who was good-hearted but totally ineffective.

"The business," he said, "was a small heavy equipment rental office in Minnesota. We rented machinery to construction companies and independent operators. I worked there my first year out of college while deciding if I wanted to go on to graduate school. I'm surprised I lasted a whole year. I guess I still thought about life in two-semester chunks.

"Mr. Abbot was middle-aged, always wore a white shirt and either a blue tie or a green one. He probably had only the two. There were five of us in the office taking orders by phone and making sure the equipment got where it was supposed to go when it was supposed to get there.

"Things were okay for the first month or so, then some of my co-workers started to complain to me about the other workers. Everybody had a complaint about somebody. Once every few weeks, Mr. Abbot would call a meeting. He would tell us not to gossip and if you had a complaint about somebody, work it out with the other person; if that didn't work, come to him. Things usually got better the next day and reverted to normal the day after that.

"I went to him once with an idea of how we might create a more effective way of scheduling. He told me it was an interesting idea. That was the last he mentioned it, and nothing changed.

"Everybody liked him. He told the funniest jokes,

remembered everyone's birthday, and gave out bonuses as often as he could. He was a nice guy; he just didn't know how to manage an office. Of course, I'd rather work for an honest friendly guy than a self-serving louse, but neither contributes much to a company bottom line or a sense of satisfaction from a job well done."

The rest of the group shared similar stories of true and not so true leaders. We all had heroes and we all had horror stories.

"So," Bob said, getting up to stand next to a whiteboard. "What does a true leader look like?"

We peppered him with concepts and spent the next hour debating what should be on the list and exactly what each characteristic meant. Rudy challenged us to distill our ideas down to only five. After significant agony, this was our list.

> A true leader:
> - Inspires
> - Acts according to clearly articulated and universal values
> - Is doggedly process oriented
> - Has a clear and clearly expressed vision
> - Listens and learns

I tell you it was like sweating blood to agree to just these five. We argued with Rudy and Bob about the five-item limit; "capricious" we called it. They said they wanted a very clear target for becoming true leaders and five was enough. If we wanted to add more when the collaborative was over, that was up to us.

Once we agreed, Rudy stood up and declared, "We have four goals for this collaborative. Number one is what you just agreed on; achieve the five most important characteristics of a true leader." That seemed like a good goal to me.

At our first break, I asked Rose why she had signed up for the Mistake-Proofing collaborative. "I want to be a mentor," she said. "I'm seventy-five years old and want to retire before I turn eighty. In the time I have left, I want to make sure every bit of wisdom I've acquired gets passed down. I don't want to teach people my bad habits. I want them to learn real skills."

Rose reminded me of my granny Jean. Both were short, less than five feet, with pure white hair. Rose was wearing a cherry red dress that looked exactly right on her. I could see her striding down the hallways at work like an intense grandmother racing to save kids from jumping off roofs or sticking forks into electric outlets.

"I expect this course will teach me how to make sure I'm teaching the right way rather than my way. It's quite exciting really. But I'm a bit afraid I might learn I've been doing it wrong for fifty years."

I laughed. "Me, too."

The second half of the morning session was surprising. I thought we'd get into how to become a true leader. Instead, we spent about ninety minutes talking about nominal leaders.

We went around the table one more time, each of us describing a personal experience with a nominal leader. John and Ann, who had presented stories of nominal leaders in the first go-around, easily came up with a second example of lousy leadership. It's everywhere like they said. Complaining about these experiences with bad leaders was kinda fun, cathartic. Then Bob lowered the boom.

"Assuming that none of you is a true leader yet, ask yourself if you are a nominal leader. What mistakes have you made and are even making now in your current position?"

We all groaned and called him unfair. But we saw the wisdom of calling a spade a spade. We were taking this collaborative to learn, so we may as well air our dirty laundry.

"Break into four groups of two," he continued. "Think about how you lead. Make a list of how you may not be perfect."

Rose and I paired up. "Shall we list our sins and transgressions?" she asked.

"Okay." I thought for a moment. "I suppose one of my limitations is I want bullet points. I'm busy. I'm in a hurry. Just give me the highlights. I probably don't get all the information available or all the information that I need. I also may not give people enough time or attention."

"That's nothing," Rose said. "In my time I've probably told ten thousand people how to do a job my way without a thought that maybe they had a better idea."

I took up her undeclared challenge. "That may be true, but I, in a shorter time, probably delegated fifteen thousand assignments with such confusing directions that Einstein couldn't have gotten them right."

Rose smiled sweetly as if I were a grandchild caught stealing a cookie. "I can believe that. Yet, do you think you've worked more twelve-hour days which, if you were smarter, could have been nine-hour days? And allowed you more time with your family? I probably wasted a decade or more."

I countered with, "Did you ever make a decision that cost your company two million dollars?"

Rose laughed. "Not all at once like you may have, but bit by bit, I'm sure I've made ten million dollars' worth of mistakes."

"I think I have let at least a dozen people leave the company because I didn't know how to get them to stay."

"And I've let dozens stay I should have let go!"

"How has American business survived? I'm surprised we still have jobs. You know Rose, this is a good exercise. It sure shows us how far we are from true leaders, how far most leaders are from true leaders."

She shrugged her shoulders. "Business goes on as usual probably because everyone else is just as bad as we have been, if not worse."

Rose and I got back on track and listed twenty-two significant weaknesses we have exhibited in our leadership. As we did that, we could hear the murmurs of the other teams. They were equally engaged and astonished at the error rate. We did another go around with both Bob and Rudy listing our faults on flip charts. While one wrote, the other asked for the next fault. Our four groups came up with 87 faults, with many overlapping, of course. We tend to make the same kind of mistakes. Bob challenged us to narrow that 87 to the ten most significant.

This discussion was even more engaging than the first because we were talking about ourselves. It was engaging and a bit unnerving. As we talked, our two facilitators kept asking us for examples of what each concept looked like in the real world. This was the reality we were bringing into the collaborative. This was us in the raw and we sure better be honest and accurate in what we were saying. It took us ninety minutes to get the list down to ten.

Nominal Leader Characteristics

Poor human-relations skills	Blames others
Poor communication skills	Failure to lead
Lack of ethics or character	Inconsistency
Failure to follow through	Poor decision making
Failure to hold staff accountable	Lack of vision

Of course, this wasn't good enough either. Rudy told us to cut it down to the five most significant nominal leader characteristics and put them into active language. "Rather than a lack of something like 'lack of ethics,' tell us what they actually do that is bad."

This was the most fruitful and enjoyable business discussion I've had in a long time. We were talking ideals and what was real at the same time. All of us had an example of the destruction caused by a nominal leader. Harriet told the story of one of the vice presidents at a local hospital she didn't want to name. The vice president, Harriet called 'Carol,' continually made executive decisions without any real understanding of the processes she was affecting.

One day Carol decided that to promote better patient satisfaction, every complaint should be recorded into a computer database. From these data, trends would be seen, and remedies found. What she didn't anticipate was the confusion over exactly what degree of complaint warranted inclusion in the database and how anyone was going to free up the time to do complaint entry, especially when some jobs like in the billing department were almost 100% complaint handling. Needless to say, this initiative fell of its own weight, there was another smudge on Carol's credibility, and nothing changed. I thought to myself, I've done that.

We got so much into storytelling and discussing what nominal leaders do that we almost ignored the lunchtime announcement; one hour on our own. The three and a half hours had gone quickly, but I was a little dazed and ready for a longer break. The eight of us around the table collected our things as we considered what to do. Rose had volunteered her company conference room as our meeting place in downtown Bellevue, convenient for everyone and within walking distance of a half-dozen good restaurants. We formed into three groups, those who were after Thai, a group that wanted Mexican and a bunch that craved wraps. Rose, Harriett, John and I were headed to the Blue Burrito, Rose in the lead.

The BB, as Rose called it, seemed to have a hundred tables with ten people at each table all talking at once. We were led to a small nook near the back that was a little quieter and more comfortable for the four of us. Settling in, perusing the menu and ordering took just a few minutes. During our first conversational lull, I asked, "So, how is it so far for everyone?"

John answered first.

"I'm pleased. I was worried that we'd just be given information, the same kind you get in a book. Instead, what we've done so far is making us think and conceptualize."

"Me, too." To be seen, Harriet had to lean around the server who was already bringing enormous and very hot plates filled to their edges. "I'm not looking for more information, I'm looking for knowledge. I like how we're all working with ideas and seeing where they take us."

I had another question. "Does anyone think Rudy and Bob can really teach us how to mistake-proof our leadership?"

Rose smiled that grandmotherly smile. "We'll see."

* * *

The afternoon began with continuing the assignment of culling our ten nominal characteristics down to five. We divided into two groups, each given half the current list and asked to redefine the characteristics and to put them into order of importance. My group was my lunch group: Rose the store owner, John the Boy Scout leader, and Harriet the state representative. We were given this list to work on:

- Poor human relations skills
- Poor communication skills
- Lack of vision
- Failure to lead
- Blames others

Rudy and Bob took turns listening to our mini-group discussions but limited their comments to helping us keep on track. The first order of business was to convert the negative into what nominal leaders did rather than didn't do. Anyone, Bob said, can have poor human relations skills, but what does that mean from someone who is a nominal leader? It wouldn't help to say a nominal leader discourages people; that would be too narrow of an effect. It also wouldn't help to say something like they negatively affect people. That was too broad to be meaningful. We had to come up with something that we could use to recognize when someone, including one of us, did it so we could mistake-proof it. This was not going to be easy. But it sure was interesting. It took close to forty minutes to redefine all five. This is what we wrote on a flip chart:

> A Nominal Leader:
> - Diminishes the value of others
> - Doesn't take responsibility for own failures
> - Sees only the immediate picture or a vague future state
> - Allows others to wander and get lost
> - Communicates too broadly or narrowly and often chooses the wrong channels

As far as order of importance was concerned, all we did was move "communicating" down two spots and "blame" toward the top. We figured that people were most important, taking responsibility second, a vision third, leading somewhere fourth and communicating fifth. We all agreed that these nominal leader characteristics should be eliminated.

Our two teams gathered together, and we reported first. There was some good discussion that changed our definitions a little but kept the same order.

The other group, Sid the coach, Susan the stay-at-home mom, Richard the Colonel and Allen the farmer from Spokane then presented their five characteristics:

> A Nominal Leader:
> - Is self-serving
> - Speaks and behaves erratically
> - Makes decisions too quickly/slowly, with inadequate information or logic
> - Allows efforts to diminish before reaching goals

This was the order they liked. They had also combined failure to hold staff accountable and failure to follow through, so we just had to reduce nine characteristics to five.

It took half-an-hour of delightful and at times heated discussion. We had a devil of a time defining what our terms meant. We decided that nominal leaders are those others depend on to lead, but who have weaknesses that significantly undermine their value as leaders, and no one does anything about it. Nominal leaders are at worst dangerous, at best creators of waste. Was that us? We struggled a bit but eventually agreed on five defining characteristics of a nominal leader.

> A Nominal Leader:
> - Treats people as a tool to get to a goal
> - Pursues a personal rather than a global vision
> - Leads by authority, not wisdom
> - Blames others

We were a bit surprised that Bob and Rudy let us get away with such vague definitions. Until Rudy went up to the whiteboard and drew a line, labeling the left end "nominal leader" and the other "true leader" and then asked us to put our name on the continuum at the point we felt we were today and an "X" at the point we'd like to get to.

"I'm not sure I can do that," Allen said before anyone could get up. "I have to hire a lot of seasonal workers to get my crop in. Is that treating people as only a tool to get to a goal? I feel that I treat them well. I don't want to put myself down as a nominal leader."

Harriett had a similar comment. "Although I want to be a good politician, I know I'm no Abe Lincoln. No one is going to miss my presence at the legislature in twenty years. Am I a nominal leader?"

We began to rebel against our own definitions. Sid added, "None of us leads by wisdom. We lead by experience, but I'm not sure about wisdom. What did we mean by wisdom anyway?"

"You all seem to be defining a nominal leader as a bad thing," Rudy said.

"Sure seems like it is," Rose told him.

"Well, you're right; Bob and I think being a nominal leader is a bad thing. We wanted you to define what a bad leader looked like. We're all bad leaders at times when we're frustrated or tired, when we're out of our element, when we just don't know how to get from point A to point B. For now, just make your best guess where on the line you think you are and an "X" where you would like to be; and know that our job in this collaborative is to move you to where you put your "X."

After we all added our marks, our continuum looked like this:

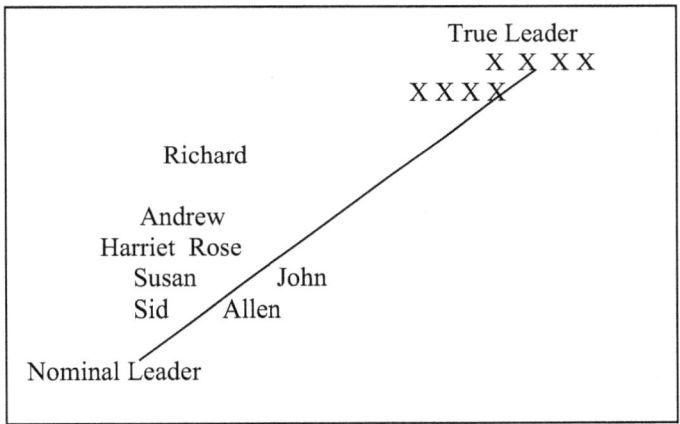

Bob stood by the board and pointed to "Richard." "It looks like the Colonel is leading our team toward true leadership. What do you have to say for yourself, Colonel?"

"That's easy. The army provided me with a lot of leadership training. We are trained to pursue our objectives with as much effort as it takes. We honor our troops and certainly have the big picture in mind even as we crawl through mud. I may be nominal at times and certainly admit I don't have yet what we might call true leadership skills, but I'm curious gentlemen; where would you put yourselves?"

28 Mistake-Proofing Leadership

Bob and Rudy rose to the challenge.

In turn, each walked up to the board, stood there a moment looking at us, and with a flourish, put their initials at the very top of the line.

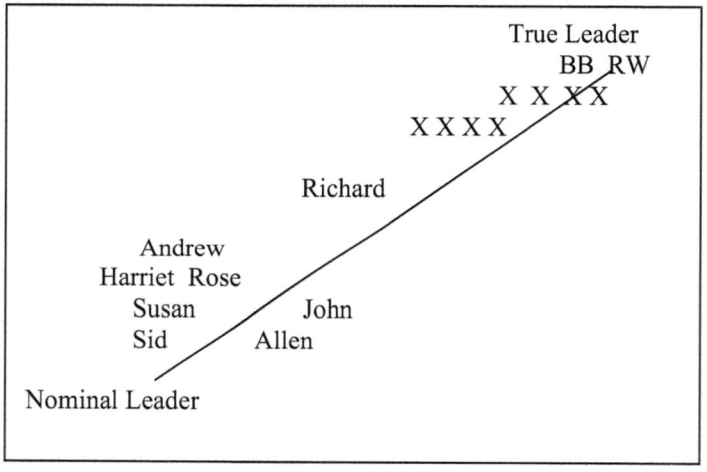

"Really?" Susan sounded like she needed convincing.

"Sure," Bob responded. "Rudy and I are proof that just about anyone can become a true leader. Not necessarily a great leader, but a true one. And we believe every great leader is a true leader. So if you can get the true leader part right, who knows how great you might become? Each of you, for example, might be remembered in twenty years like my Dr. Carrie, or even long after that. But as intriguing as this is, it's time to move on. What we want to accomplish this afternoon is for all of you to have a very clear idea of how to become a true leader. We want you to leave this afternoon knowing exactly how a true leader is different from everyone else."

Rudy took over. "You may be wondering why we titled this collaborative 'Mistake-Proofing Leadership.' The reason is simple. For most of us, being a true leader is not something we can achieve easily. As you demonstrated, even at your fairly advanced levels of experience and skill, you all chose to define yourselves closer to being a nominal leader than a true leader. That doesn't happen by accident, and ironically it shows that you are closer to being true leaders than you indicated.

For the most part, nominal leaders don't know how inadequate they are, while most good leaders know what their weaknesses are, but may not know how to get better. All of you are in the latter category.

You all told stories of poor leaders who had no clue they were poor leaders. And most of you had stories of true leaders who had significant impact on you and others. Bob and I think that with one simple concept, you all can become true leaders: mistake-proof your leadership, which means you no longer make damaging leadership mistakes. You don't need to be a great leader, but your leadership does need to be mistake-proofed.

Think about this. If you suddenly became sick and needed a doctor, would you stay with one who said, "To tell the truth, I generally don't do well with your particular problem, but I'd sure be glad to give you my best effort." Of course, you wouldn't. Now think of your employees who depend on you for leadership and you just admitted that you make quite a few mistakes. Is that what you want? Is that what they want? Is that the best you can do?"

Dear old Rose had to interrupt. "I wondered what this was really all about. Are you saying that we can actually mistake-proof our leadership?"

Bob answered simply, "Yes, we are."

Rudy added, "But not by yourself. People cannot be perfect by themselves. No one is ever going to be without flaw. No leader is going to lead without making mistakes. But processes can be created and set in place where mistakes are identified and fixed before they do any harm. To continue our medical metaphor, if baby delivery in the United States was performed at a 99.9% perfection rate, obstetricians would accidentally drop forty newborns a day. Not a good situation. But since these are visible errors, we can figure out what caused the babies to slip and fix the problem. Leaders make a lot of decisions that are harder to judge. Sometimes it's impossible to immediately see if an error occurred. It might take years to see how a decision ultimately turns out. We need ways to anticipate and head off the potential harm resulting from leader mistakes.

Conceptually, mistake-proofing leadership is simple. If you as a leader can identify what should be done based on sound principles and do it, there's no problem. When you know what should be done, don't do it but quickly notice the omission, you usually can still fix it in time to avoid harm. And, if your followers know what you should do and you have granted them enough influence to correct your leadership errors, they also will help ensure mistake-proofed leadership."

Rose raised her hand and began talking as soon as Rudy looked at her. "Rudy, I've been around a long time. I've seen more leadership theories come and go than Carters has pills. I'm here because I want to learn what mistake-proofing leadership is all about." She shook her head. "We're all human here. Are you really saying that you can make all of us mistake-proofed leaders?" It sounded like the same question she asked earlier.

Rudy's answer was emphatic. "Yes."

Rose was startled. "'Yes.' That's all you have to say? No equivocation?"

"One equivocation."

Rose smiled. "I thought so."

"It won't happen overnight. There is no magic way of never making a mistake again, but, and this is a very important but, leaders can lead in a way that gets better every day and minimizes weaknesses, improves strengths, and, last but not least, encourages unleashing the leadership of everyone involved. The long-term goal is to mistake-proof leadership or in other words, eliminate harm caused by faulty leadership. It can't get better than that."

Richard the Colonel raised his hand. "So, you're saying that we can learn how to be better every day from now on and every day get closer to being mistake-proofed?"

Bob answered this one along the same vein Rudy did, "Yes. And there's more." He tried to sound like one of those TV commercials. "And not only do you get to improve every day, minimize weaknesses and improve strengths but if you act now, you'll also receive a way of measuring progress and you'll also be training your staff how to be true leaders just like you."

"So far," Rudy continued, "we've talked about true and nominal leaders. Does everyone have a good idea of what a true leader is?" We all nodded. "Good. How about nominal leaders? We all nodded again. "Good." He looked at his watch. "In our last hour, we want to cover how to become a true leader. Bob?"

Bob stood up and walked to a far corner of the room. Then he began pretending to shoot a basketball. At least that's what it looked like. He did whatever he was doing for about half a minute. "I'm shooting free throws," he said. "What needs to happen for me to improve?"

Susan immediately said, "Feedback. You need to know if you're making them or how you're missing them."

Bob stopped. "Perfect," he said. "The only way to improve something is to get feedback on your performance. That is true of leadership, too. What else do I need in order to improve?"

This one had us stumped for a moment. Sid, the coach, came through like a champ. "Technique or skills. You need to know how to shoot and how to improve. You need to know how to improve your technique."

Bob looked over to Rudy. "Boy, am I glad we invited these people."

Rudy jumped in, "And that's what mistake-proofing leadership involves, skills and feedback. We're going to teach you the best practice leadership skills and enable you to know how well you're using them. Form into three groups. I'll join one so each group has three people, and Bob will visit each one as a coach. What we want you to do in your group is identify and discuss any assumptions you have about leadership skills and competencies. We want you to discuss what you know right now about how to become a better leader. The reason for this exercise is to clear up any erroneous assumptions and ensure that we all see the bright white line between nominal leaders and true leaders."

Harriett, Allen and I pulled our chairs together into a small circle. I wouldn't have believed it if someone had said our group would talk nonstop for forty minutes. But we did. We had only fifteen minutes left when the whole group got together again.

"What did you come up with?" Bob asked.

Allen spoke for our group. "Leadership is something you can be born with, it's in our personality, but it can also be developed. It's harder for some than for others. Leadership is complicated and slow to grow. I guess we didn't go deep into the subject, but that's about it for our group."

Richard went next for his group. "We talked a bit about what

Allen mentioned. We think leadership is something that can add to itself. That is if you're successful leading one thing you are likely to be good at leading the next thing, and people are going to be more willing to follow. We also think that to be a good leader you probably have to learn how to be a good follower. A tightly defined structure of when you're a leader and when you're a follower seems to help."

"Like in the army," John called out.

"Yes," Richard agreed, "like the army. We also talked about how helpful it is to be allowed to make mistakes. We think developing leaders should stretch themselves, fail at times, but hopefully not so there is any permanent damage to anyone."

"We agree to all of the above," Susan spoke for her group. "We would also add that for a leader to grow he or she must want to. We had Rudy in our group as a ringer and he mentioned expectancy theory where people need to expect that they will have a positive effect before they'll try something. Growing leaders is the same thing. Leaders must figure that the effort is worth making and that the result is going to be meaningful. We talked about great leaders being great leaders because they accomplished great things. We liked the idea of leaders being true leaders because they accomplished true things. Last, we liked the idea of a flat leadership structure where everyone is a leader to some degree."

Bob walked over to the flip chart that listed our objectives. "We know what true leaders are. We know what nominal leaders are. Do we also know that to become a true leader we must have…" and he started writing on another flip chart.

> To Become a True Leader, We Must:
> - Have the best leadership skills
> - Get constant feedback
> - Be highly motivated
> - Have lofty goals that make the effort worthwhile
> - Know when to lead and when to follow
> - Have confidence that we will be able to reach our goal
> - Be willing to make mistakes – but not horrible ones
> - Maximize the leadership of everyone
> - Act from a set of universal values

Bob turned to us. "Agreed?"

We finished reading the list and agreed.

Rudy stood up. "Next time, next week at noon actually, back here at Rose's place – and thank you Rose for being our host for our first two meetings – we will jump into the four pillars of mistake-proofing that form the structure for everything else we do: moments of truth, the concept of waste, mistake-proofing, and bundling. In two hours, we're going to cover the meat and potatoes of mistake-proofing leadership so when we're finished you won't be able to sleep until you actually begin mistake-proofing your leadership. Any questions?"

There were none. I think all of us were mentally fatigued. It had only been from eighty-thirty until three-thirty with an hour for lunch, but I don't think I've put as many brains cells to work in a long time and probably no one else had either.

"How did it go today?" Bob asked.

"Great. Super. Very informative. Exactly what I was hoping for." All the comments framed our enthusiasm.

"How could it have gone better?" Rudy asked.

We mulled that one over. None of us had anything negative to say so we all made more comments about how much we had gained.

"Thank you all for coming," Bob said. "And remember, next week we cover the four pillars of mistake-proofing leadership. You'll be too excited to sleep until you put the ideas into action."

3

THE FOUR PILLARS

We had an assignment to report on: *Observe leaders within your organizations or elsewhere and assess if they are using any form of best practices in their leadership. Prepare to report on one of them.*

The assignment was deliberately vague as to exactly what we were looking for, but I think each of us had a good idea. I decided to use as a template the example of airline pilots who follow strict procedures for take-offs and landings and probably everything in between. It would be immediately clear to everyone if any pilot decided to be creative. "Good morning, folks, this is your captain speaking. We're about to land at Las Vegas and in the true spirit of gambling, I'll roll the dice, multiply by fifty knots and try to bring 'er down at that speed. What de ya say?" Pilots use best practices, but I'm not sure many leaders do. Only one day after our first meeting I knew who I would report on.

I would report on me.

We assembled again in Rose's conference room. Rudy said he would start us off with a story about knowing exactly what to do exactly when it needed to be done. No second-guessing, no 'almost' knowing, no room for error. He stood at the end of the table and began. It was about a pilot!

"It was 6:45 on a sunny California July morning. Wanda, my flight student, was sitting in the left seat of my Cessna 150, ready for her second flying lesson. We had completed the pre-flight and pre-takeoff checklists, scanned the pattern for other aircraft, and taxied onto the narrow runway. I could sense her growing excitement. I advanced the throttle and the engine roared. We bounced along gaining speed and then lifted free of the runway. Wanda was thrilled. Everything was perfect. That is until we reached 350 feet. Suddenly, the plane shook violently. Our engine had failed. We were going down! What to do?

"Having taught other flight students exactly what to do, I did just what I taught: Lower the nose to the best glide speed, pull carb heat to melt any carburetor ice, check the fuel system, and select a landing site. Do not try a 180-degree turn back to the runway; too low to make it. With grape vineyards on the left and alfalfa fields with irrigation ridges running the wrong way on the right and straight ahead, our only decent choice was a tiny undulating cow pasture about 45 degrees off the nose to the right. But could we stay up long enough to clear the railroad tracks, telephone lines and tall trees? We re-tightened our seatbelts and harnesses. Then, the second we cleared the trees, we lowered the nose, dropped our flaps, turned off the electrical system, and cracked open the doors. The last two in case this became a crash instead of an off-airport landing.

"We touched down as smoothly as possible on the rough surface and rolled safely to a stop. The standard procedures worked! As we walked back to the airport, I realized that Wanda was not at all upset. She had done everything she needed to do and treated the entire emergency as a normal part of flying. Later that year, she completed her private license. And over the next several years she continued to take lessons from me, earning commercial, instrument, and multiengine ratings, and finally a flight instructor certificate. She later flew spotter planes for California's aerial firefighting bombers."

Rudy's story was a great introduction to my report, but I didn't want to go first again. Let someone else have a chance. Allen, who admirably drove the 280 miles from Spokane and planned to drive it every week, volunteered to begin.

"I understood the assignment was to observe a leader and determine if the leader seemed to have a plan or system for what he did. Well, I'm the leader that I can observe the most, so I observed me."

I laughed. So did everyone else.

"I'm just curious," Bob said. "How many of you are going to

report about yourself as a leader?"

Everyone raised a hand. Maybe that's what they intended.

We all gave our seven-minute presentation using different words and different examples, but all concluding that we mostly led reactively based on our experience, intuition and best guesses; and not much based on models or explicit theory. None was sure what kind of feedback would tell us if we were leading well or if people were just putting up with us.

Rudy looked over to Bob and in a stage whisper said, "I think we have the right group." Then in a normal voice added, "You all just demonstrated one of the three elements of mistake-proofing, which we will discuss in a bit. But we promised you the four pillars of mistake-proofing leadership today along with considerable excitement and motivation, so we better get to it. Bob and I believe that understanding and applying the four pillars is the best way to be a true leader. We'll start with 'Moments of Truth.' Bob's a golfer so he loves to introduce this concept."

Bob stood up and walked to the whiteboard. At the top, he wrote "Moment of Truth." "A moment of truth," he said, "is any moment when you make a considered decision that has consequences and involves values. A moment of truth is not deciding which cereal to pour into a bowl at seven a.m. It is a decision that exposes your character, defines what you stand for, and affects you or others in significant ways. And yet, it often is not a major decision.

"Golfers, for example, are responsible for their own score. In most matches, the only one who knows a golfer's score for sure is that golfer. A classic example of the honor that golf is famous for is when a golfer is just about to putt and the ball moves. Even if no one saw the ball move and even if the player didn't make it move, the golfer is expected to report the movement to the other players and self-assess a penalty stroke. The same is true if the player is alone deep in the woods, swings at the ball and misses. When the golfer emerges from the trees, every swing, good and bad, is expected to be counted and reported. The moment of truth is when the golfer could do the right thing and does or doesn't. A small thing as far as a golf score is concerned, but it means everything about character.

"In business, a moment of truth can be a customer service concept. Any time a customer has an expectation of your business and interacts with your employees or product there is a moment of truth: Will customer expectations be met or not?

"Leadership is also defined by moments of truth. You often need to make a decision without adequate information. A meeting you're running can go in one direction or another. You have an opportunity to bury bad news or divulge it. All moments of truth.

"There are obvious ingredients in moments of truth. First, recognize that you're facing one. Then understand your options. To make the decision you need a value system and the courage to decide consistent with those values. And you better monitor the consequences and be willing to face another moment of truth if things aren't going well.

"Leadership, like life, is a series of choices. Part of being a true leader is being able to recognize when a choice is significant, a moment of truth, and make the right decision. And if you don't make the right decision, to be able to minimize damage and, we hope, recover well."

Bob then wrote on the board:

> **Moment of Truth**
> - A choice needs to be made
> - Values are involved
> - Consequences are significant
> - You are the decision maker

"Does this make sense to everyone?"

John raised his hand to speak. "This is what Scouting is all about. We try to teach kids to do the right thing. Often, they struggle with what they want to do against what they know they should do. Scout leaders provide these young people with an external frame of reference that guides them during their moments of truth."

Sid couldn't help adding, "I'm thinking of all those recent business scandals. An external frame of reference could have saved a lot of those older businessmen." He looked over to Harriett, "And saved a lot of not so good politicians."

"I couldn't agree more," Harriett said. "A moral compass is a necessity if you want to do anything right."

"So, one pillar," Bob continued, "of true leadership is self-awareness and enough awareness of the big picture to know when a moment of truth has arrived and know what to do about it. We'll get into this much more as we go on. In fact, later today our look at self-awareness should be enlightening."

I had a question. "I get that we all face moments of truth and those of us with good character have a better chance of making good decisions. I can see that if an employee is facing a customer and makes a short-sighted decision that doesn't satisfy the customer, that it is a missed moment of truth. Tell me what a nominal leader does at a moment of truth and how that differs from a true leader. What's the difference?"

"Effective leadership," Bob said, "is dependent on how you perceive the situation. Nominal leaders put themselves at the center of the issue. Decisions are based on the ultimate consequences suffered or enjoyed by the leader such as getting into trouble or looking bad. Nominal leaders may see the big picture but operate from personal gain. True leaders, on the other hand, are driven by a meaning greater than themselves. Decisions are made for the greater good not just personal benefit.

"Both nominal and true leaders sometimes make the same decision, but rarely for the same reasons. Think of it this way: if a nominal leader faces a moment of truth, you can never trust that the outcome will be the right one. When a true leader faces a moment of truth, you can always trust that the leader's intent will support the greater good. As we said at our first meeting, true leadership is obvious. This is one of those times that even if you do not see the difference, you'll sense it."

Rudy stood up. "Does everyone understand the moment of truth concept?" We all nodded our heads. "Moments of truth always demand a reference point greater than one's self: truth. Can we see the truth or only our own needs? One of the reasons we call true leaders 'true' is that they remain true to the positive values that they and we espouse. They act from a perspective that is value-added. We'll add vision to this concept a bit later. For now, let's look at…"

Harriett had raised her hand. "Rudy, before you continue, could you give us a couple of examples of nominal leaders?"

"Sure. Since you're a politician, let's do some of those. Just about any dictator is a nominal leader. Horrendous acts have been committed by many of these nominal leaders in their quest to stay in power. 'Pork barrel' additions to legitimate bills in the legislature point to nominal leadership." Harriett smiled a rueful smile.

Rudy continued. "Bob and I once had a long discussion about elected leaders who garner less than a majority approval rating being nominal leaders unless they resign their office. But then some leaders are unpopular because they've made unpopular but right decisions, so it's problematic to judge a true leader by vote.

"It is also simplistic to declare someone a nominal leader just because they are culturally different, and we don't share the same values. Cultural norms are important and can't be ignored, but any culture or even government that promotes ruthless self-serving behaviors and an us-against-them philosophy, or any form of elitism, results in nominal leadership."

Harriett wanted to know more. "So only a true leader acts from the perspective of higher values?"

"Yes. One way to judge a leader during a moment of truth is to decide if the behavior is consistent with higher values. But even that requires informed judgment. Does that help?"

"Yes, thank you."

"All right. Let's jump into pillar number two, eliminating waste through Lean Thinking. Nominal leaders create much more waste when they attempt to lead than do true leaders. A leader making decisions is like a boat cruising through the organization creating a wake of messages and actions others must address. During the Korean War, Lean thinking Taiichi Ohno of the extraordinarily successful Toyota Production System, found himself running a production plant with a decreasing number of workers. A simple formula drove his effort to increase efficiency."

Rudy wrote the formula on the whiteboard.

> Present capacity = work + waste

"From this simple equation, you can see that whatever we accomplish is the result of both our value-adding effort and the waste of our mistakes.

"A leader's capacity to put forth effort to accomplish great things is equal to a leader's true leadership effort plus his or her nominal leadership effort; i.e., productive effort plus mistakes. Given the same effort expended, the fewer the errors the greater the productive leadership. The formula applies to leadership as well as to an assembly line.

"Taiichi Ohno identified seven wastes that we can easily apply to leadership. We added the eighth which Bob Emiliani, author of *Better Thinking, Better Results*, explores in detail. The examples are ours."

Rudy then went to his table and pulled out this large poster. He made a show of struggling to carry it to the front of the room and attempted to tape it to the wall. Bob rushed over and helped him put it up. Rudy sighed in relief.

"This is only a small example of what we are up against when we decide to become a leader. It is a profound responsibility that most leaders fail to grasp and appreciate."

He gave us time to read it before continuing.

Types of Waste Leaders Create

1. **Time** – Makes staff wait too long for opportunities to discuss problems and get decisions they need.

2. **Processing** – Uses an ineffective, inefficient problem-solving methodology.

3. **Motion** – Has to search too much for what is needed instead of having work related items easily at hand.

4. **Defects** – Makes poor decisions that violate staff or customer expectations. Delegates poorly and then needs to do rework to correct the errors.

5. **Transportation** – Requires too many reports to go from office to office to receive required but unnecessary signatures. Requires too many in-person check-ins by staff before they go to the next step.

6. **Inventory** – Allows unneeded resources to accumulate, including materials, equipment and people.

7. **Overproduction** – Requires too much data, too many detailed reports and too little real meaning. Uses more measures than are needed to evaluate a project's progress.

8. **Behaviors** – Relies too much on threat and position power which causes uncertainty, fear and confusion in staff. Does not apply lean principles to leadership.

"Bob Emiliani notes that Lean Thinking contains two important principles: respect for people and continuous improvement by eliminating waste. Both of these are also hallmarks of The Toyota Way. Without both, success will be difficult, perhaps impossible. Just as Ohno classified work as value-added or non-value added, Emiliani did the same with leadership. He defined behavioral waste as 'behaviors that add cost but do not add value to products or services: stereotyping, bullying, being inaccessible, fomenting confusion, office politics, unknown expectations, saying one thing and doing another, inability to admit errors, and blaming people for problems.' How's that for defining nominal leadership? To become a true leader, you must eliminate waste from your leadership and enhance leadership assets."

Allen raised his hand. "And you're going to tell us how right?"

"Right," Rudy answered. "But not all of it today. So far, we've touched on two ideas, moments of truth and eliminating waste from your leadership. Good ideas? Are you getting excited to get out there and experience moments of truth and eliminate leadership waste?"

We all nodded and said, "Yeah, let's get to it."

"Are you ready?" Rudy asked louder.

"We're ready," we answered.

"Are you ready?" he cried.

"We're ready!" We shouted.

"No, you're not," Bob said.

Most of us booed.

"Hold on," he said. "How many of you are familiar with the concept of Lean Thinking that Rudy just mention?"

Only three of us held up our hands.

"Is it okay with you three if we do a review of Lean principles so the others can catch up?" We agreed, of course. It's always a good idea to review Lean principles; many of them are counterintuitive. Rudy and Bob then did an excellent job of covering the five principles: Value, Value Stream, Flow, Pull and Perfection. It was less a presentation than asking us about our work and applying Lean principles to what we did. For example, we talked about value being defined by the end-use customer and a value stream as the steps needed to transform raw material into a finished product placed in the hands of a customer.

Susan, the stay at home mother, was a great example of the value stream. Rudy said, "In Susan's value stream her customer could be the world and her product her two sons. As a parent, Susan has the job of adding value to her sons as they grow. Everything you do as a mother, Susan, adds value to your children or it doesn't. Their development is the value stream. Your job is to add value as it goes along. True value can only be determined by the ultimate customer. In the case of your sons, it's the world."

Susan caught on quickly and said, "It's also true that my kids are the ultimate customer of my parenting. They decide if I add value to their lives or not."

Sid added, "Then it is probably true that a leader adds value to the world or doesn't and adds value for followers or doesn't. Right?"

We discussed this idea without additional comment from our two leaders and had a great time. Finally, Bob interrupted. "A value stream includes all the activities from the start of something until the conclusion. These activities can be value-added, non-value-added-but-necessary, or waste. Non-value-added-but-necessary are activities like monitoring employee timecards, at least until the process is mistake-proofed. Everybody got that?"

We did.

"Who can describe a leadership value stream that has waste in it?"

John took the plunge. "Say a leader is gathering information to make a decision. The leader can gather way more than is necessary or ignore important information. Is this what you're looking for?"

"Exactly what we're looking for. That's an example of processing waste. Who has another example?"

I had one. "How about when a leader leads somewhere that isn't a useful place to be? Like to produce an Edsel that nobody wants?"

"Perfect. If we don't produce what a customer wants, we're not upholding the first Lean principle, value defined by the customer. And when we remove waste, we honor the second principle that differentiates value-added from non-value-added activities."

"The next two Lean principles are called flow and pull. Flow means that raw materials, information and parts move along smoothly like in Allen's irrigation ditches after he removes the weeds, soil and other obstructions. And pull means that nothing is done until the customer asks for it. You don't manufacture a car until the dealer gets an order. And during the manufacturing process, a part isn't made until the downstream assembly station orders it. Things are pulled not pushed."

"It's like when I grow crops," Allen said. "I have a pretty good idea what the demand is going to be before I plant. I don't just hope someone will buy what I grow; I make sure to set things up as well as I can so there is a customer ready and waiting when the crops come in."

"Politics is similar, and I suppose different, too," said Harriett. "I respond to my constituents, that's my job, but I also have to anticipate potential problems and deal with them before they become actual problems. I guess that's what farmers do, too. You worry about pests and drought and make sure you're prepared to take care of the problems as soon as they begin."

Farmer Allen agreed. "That's right. I try to anticipate flow problems so I can meet the pull expectations of my customer."

Rudy re-entered the conversation, "Okay Lean Thinking experts, we know that a Lean process is designed to add value for the customer, minimize waste, and make sure things flow smoothly at the pace determined by customer pull. And although we haven't said much yet about people behavior causing waste, people behaviors are a critical part of Lean. Given all that, what would you say is the ultimate goal of Lean Thinking?"

Good old Rose was equal to the task. "Perfection, boys. Perfection is the goal."

"That's it." Rudy pointed both index fingers at her. "Lean Thinking is a process that strives to eliminate waste bit by bit until every action along the value stream adds value and the customer gets the exact product desired at the absolute least possible cost. And the product, by the way, is without flaw. Bob and I believe that this process can be applied to leadership. Excited?"

We chorused, "Yes."

"There's more."

Rudy sat down and Bob stood up. "So far we have two pillars supporting true leadership: (1) moments of truth and (2) eliminating waste through Lean. Our next pillar is really cool. It combines aspects of Lean Thinking and moments of truth into something called mistake-proofing.

"Mistake-proofing is designing a way to do something that at its best prevents making mistakes and at worst identifies and corrects mistakes before they get passed on as defects to a customer. In its purest form, mistake-proofing means that the process is designed so mistakes cannot be made. For our purposes, mistake-proofing also will include ensuring mistakes are identified and fixed before they become defects, problems for followers, for customers, for the world.

"Shall we go on?" Without waiting for an answer, Bob erased the whiteboard and wrote:

Mistake-Proofing	
Poka Yoke	Right way only
Self-check	Notice and fix
Successive check	Others notice, stop the line and give feedback upstream

"The idea is that there are three ways to make sure a mistake doesn't cause a defect. The best way is to design a poka yoke, a Japanese term pronounced 'poke a yo kay,' It means impossible to make the mistake. Remember 'Murphy's Law?' If something can go wrong, it will go wrong? Poka yokes are designed to overcome Murphy's Law. The machine or process is designed to do the job exactly right; there is no other way. A simple example is a hose connection. You could design a hose connection so only the two hoses that should be connected can be connected.

"The second way of avoiding a mistake getting to the customer is self-check. The operator (in this case the leader) knows exactly what he or she should do, notices when it is done incorrectly, fixes the error and does not pass it on.

"Third is the successive check. If the person who made the error doesn't notice it, those immediately affected by the error do and refuse to pass it on. In an assembly process, suppose the worker notices that an error was passed on from upstream. What should the worker do? How many of you say, 'Fix it?'" Five of us raised our hands. "Wrong. The worker will usually stop the assembly process, gather upstream workers, and determine why the error occurred so whatever caused it can be fixed before the same error is made again. Wouldn't it be great if when a leader made an error that followers would inform the leader, so it never happened again? That's what we're going to explore."

It was Richard's turn to be brilliant. "What you're saying is interesting and very difficult. If the general gives an order, no private is going to countermand it. And certainly, no great general would want to make a mistake that could be corrected by a lowly private. But that's the idea isn't it, making sure the right thing is done no matter who thinks about it. A true leader is more interested in the result than in the glory attached to the result. I'm thinking of Lao-Tsu who said that when the best leader's work is done, the people say, 'We did it ourselves.'"

Then it was Rudy's turn. "That's exactly right. The only way to mistake-proof leadership is for the leader to ensure that poka yoke, self-check and successive check are fully operational. That isn't easy."

Rudy looked at his watch. "We have just enough time to introduce our fourth pillar, bundling."

"Is that where leaders bundle up in a suit of armor?" Sid asked, looking around for someone to laugh. No one did. "Sorry,

I couldn't contain myself."

Rudy helped him out. "Actually, that's close to the truth. Bundling is knowing what works beforehand and doing whatever that is. All of it, not missing even one necessary ingredient, just like putting on every piece of armor. You know what happened to Achilles when his heel wasn't protected.

"Here's what we mean by bundling. It is identifying all the actions that are needed for optimal results and making sure to do all of them. Not three of five or even four of five. We're talking five of five. All of them. Medicine is doing great at bundling treatments.

"As an example, let me read you the five steps in an evidenced-based medical bundle designed to eliminate ventilator caused infections: Step 1, raise the hospital bed 30-degrees so the patient sits up. Failure to raise the bed the required number of degrees is a failure to complete the bundle and success can go down; Step 2, daily sedation vacations; Step 3, daily assessment of readiness to extubate; Step 4, DVT prophylaxis, and Step 5, GI prophylaxis. Omit just one of them and the patient's treatment is compromised.

"There are also many other bundles focused on heart attacks, surgical site infections, central line infections, and so forth. I don't pretend to understand all the medical terms, but I do know that bundles work.

"So, just like medicine, leadership has bundles. Failure to use the complete bundle is a failure of leadership. Make sense?"

We all nodded.

"Do you know what the leadership bundles are?"

We all said "No."

"Well, that's why Bob and I are here."

Bob pointed to the flip chart.

> ### The Four Pillars
> 1. Moments of truth
> 2. Eliminating waste through Lean
> 3. Mistake-proofing
> 4. Leadership bundles

Are you jazzed?"

"Yes."

"Are you excited?"

"Yes."

"Can you wait for next week?"

"No."

"Told you that you wouldn't be able to wait, and we didn't even cover when to lead and when not to lead."

* * *

What a great meeting. Mistake-proofing. Leadership bundles.

Moments of truth. Eliminating waste. We spent the few remaining minutes going over our next assignment. I walked out with Allen. He was just as excited as I was. Everything made sense, good, solid practical sense. "I have a lot to think about on my drive home," he said. "Me, too," I told him. "See you next week."

4

PONDERING

We leaders don't ponder as much as we should. I've already confessed to living life by bullet points, and now I'm confessing that I don't ponder. Taking any more time than is necessary to make a decision seems like wasting time. However, our assignment after the second meeting was to ponder. We were to ponder when we should lead and when we should follow.

At first, that seemed like a no-brainer. Lead when you're the best to lead, don't lead when you're not the best to lead. This, of course, led to the problem of defining exactly when those times are. It led to wondering what the difference is between leading and following. It also slipped me into pondering about pondering.

If I ponder at all, it is probably while doing something else that doesn't require my full attention. I seem to ponder while driving and while on hold if I'm not also working on the computer.

I don't think I've ever actually sat in a chair with the intention of doing nothing but ponder. At least not until Saturday afternoon when I did exactly that. I sat in a recliner in the family room, TV off, radio off, no one around, no book in my lap, nothing else to do. I was set to ponder.

I first tackled following. When should I be a follower? I immediately realized that I didn't like the feel of that. I knew I had to follow sometimes, but that was mostly out of necessity. To choose to be a follower didn't feel right.

So I switched to thinking about being a good follower as a prerequisite to being a good leader. A leader who had been a good follower ought to be sensitive to what made following worthwhile. Being a good follower requires discipline to follow and trust that the leader is a good leader leading to the right outcome. And I suppose being a good leader requires the same type of discipline to keep the goal foremost while appreciating the cost to followers of getting there. Importantly, followers have to lead themselves by making conscious decisions to follow, in part based on their belief that they are making a needed contribution. Wise leaders reinforce this belief.

Followers benefit from belonging to a greater whole and being a contributing part of an important mission, however small or large. They enjoy feeling confident that their leader is likely to lead them to success. I sensed a synergy, an important connection, between follower and leader I hadn't appreciated before. Not an earth-shattering conclusion from my pondering, but interesting.

But what if a seemingly good leader turned out to be a bad leader? At what point should followers mutiny? When does Susan in bookkeeping have the right and even the obligation to bring down the skimming-off-the-top CFO?

In highly authoritarian organizations based more on power and gain than on integrity-based values, Susan probably wouldn't do anything, maybe quit if she worried about being implicated, but otherwise, she'd remain mum. In an organization without integrity-based values, Susan wouldn't care. She might even skim off some for herself; after all, everyone else is doing it. So, it seemed to me that the leader-follower relationship is partly determined by the values of the organization. Again, not earth-shattering, just interesting.

My attention then turned from followership to true leadership, particularly the ability to influence others. How do leaders influence others besides using their position authority or outright manipulation?

Painting a picture of the future came immediately to mind. A true leader can see and describe the future in ways that make it real, attractive, important and achievable. My mind dwelled on that idea for quite a while. It seemed to me that if a leader painted the right picture of the future, followers would flock to join. But first, a budding leader must gain the attention of potential followers.

Then I thought about the power of a good idea to guide

people versus the effort of a leader to lead. Do followers more readily follow the idea or the leader? I believe that people follow a charismatic leader with a mediocre idea more often than they follow a dull leader with a great idea.

Do I do that? I did in high school and college. I wanted to be like the cool kids. Fortunately, I've mostly grown out of that, but I suppose that many people haven't. Maybe part of maturity is choosing better leaders to follow.

How much better does an opposing idea have to be to overpower a charismatic leader who offers a mediocre idea? My hypothesis is that a leader who paints a compelling picture of the future will remain influential if he or she does not impede progress toward that future.

Leader transgressions will be judged by how much they shake follower beliefs. Small errors by a powerful leader may not shake followers. Larger errors in relation to a grand future also may have little impact on follower support. This suggests significant resilience by followers and a great deal of faith in their leader and the desired future.

Followers seem willing to sacrifice as long as there is movement toward the desired future. I thought this was interesting because it illuminates the responsibility a true leader has to followers who risk much on faith and can forgive almost to the point of self-destruction.

As unjust as it seems, the only time mutiny is a distinct

possibility for the majority of followers is when there is a potentially greater leader in the wings, a greater probable future with someone different, or a combination of both, plus a significant flaw in the current leader.

I wondered if leaders should be expected to provide a disclaimer to followers. If so, what would the disclaimer look like? A shrug of the shoulders and a "Sorry I got us into this mess." Or should leaders be held more accountable? Either provide explicit measures of progress or get out of the way?

Like an investment, leadership should promise something positive. True leadership is not against something, but for something. And true leadership must provide something for everyone.

My pondering led me to think how little I understood those who worked for me.

This troubled me enough that I took a short break and fixed myself a cup of tea. When I sat again cup in hand, I allowed myself to form some conclusions.

When should I lead? I should lead when I have confidence that I can get me and my followers to a better future. I should lead when I understand and appreciate the sacrifices my followers will make. I should lead when followers have made conscious decisions to follow and know as clearly as possible the risks and rewards. I should lead when I can articulate or demonstrate my values clearly enough that my followers can make an informed choice to follow or not follow. I should lead when I'm willing to demand an investment by followers.

When should I follow? I should follow only when someone else can be a better leader. How about when I don't care much about the outcome? No. If I don't care, why bother getting involved?

The whirring of the garage door opening told me my family had returned: Time to stop pondering and return to their world.

I'm not sure exactly how this pondering works, but I ended with a greater awareness of how important leadership is. People entrust their futures with me. They give me huge chunks of their time, their effort and their quest for doing something of value. I am in a position to change their worlds and with their help the one I live in, too. Sadly, I've been shooting too much from the hip.

Yes, followers make the decision to follow, but if I decide to lead and if I expect to be a good leader, I must honor my responsibility to those who follow. The promised future must be a good one. The plan must be well considered. My effort must be robust. I must be worthy of those I lead.

Can I become a true leader? I wasn't at all sure. What did a true leader need to know? Frankly, I ended the pondering session more than a little concerned. Can just anyone do this? Probably not. Who am I to think I can become a true leader?

5

THE ZEN OF LEADERSHIP

Sweet old Rose and I were having coffee after the fourth collaborative session. So far, the collaborative had covered everything I had ever thought about leadership and a great deal more. Rose was telling me about her leadership ideas.

"You know," she said, "leadership is like that Zen idea of 'first there is a mountain, then there is no mountain, then there is.'"

"Isn't that from a 70s Donovan song?"

"Perhaps, but it originally came from Buddhist thinking about how we understand things. When you first encounter something, all you see is the simple picture; like when you look at a mountain all you see is a very big hill. The more you look the more you learn, and the more you learn the greater detail you see. As you study a mountain, you begin to see rock formations, know what they are made of and how they were formed. You learn about watersheds, ecosystems, the tree line, microclimates and a hundred other things. As your understanding grows you see how these elements fit together and eventually, you see the entire mountain again."

"You see a mountain, then the details, then the mountain again," I said, sagely.

"Doesn't sound like much, does it? It's like another saying, 'Before enlightenment, I chopped wood and carried water. After enlightenment, I chop wood and carry water.'"

"I get the idea," I said. "With leadership, it's simple at first because we don't really know how to judge how we're doing. We may not be aware of making a mistake that alienates our employees, so we blame them for a bad attitude, not ourselves for what we may have done. Then we take classes and learn skills on the job and notice how to do things differently. We follow models and theories and do things we memorized how to do. When we have enough knowledge and experience, we make it simple again."

"I think leadership develops from ignorance to skillful to wise."

I nodded agreement. "Do you think we all start from ignorance?"

"I did," she answered, "and I think everybody does whether they admit it or not. Oh, I know that some people seem to be natural-born leaders, but I think that is more assertive temperament than good leadership. You can push a cart or pull a cart, and I think so-called natural leaders know how to push, but not so many know how to pull.

I remember back in high school I worked in a grocery store after school and on weekends. By the time I was a senior I was an assistant, assistant manager with three or four younger clerks to get the work done. I cajoled, I pleaded, I threatened, anything to get them to do the work. It got done, but only because I kept at them. It was a simple matter of brute force focused on the outcome. I didn't want to get yelled at or disappoint my boss, so I pushed and kept pushing. Many leaders never deviate from pushing toward a goal. In fact, they commend themselves for doing so; they think force is power, but in the long run, it's not efficient and it's not good leadership."

"Would you say managers do the pushing, and leaders do the pulling?"

"Not exactly. I think both managers and leaders are charged with getting the work done. They need to meet objectives, one of which should be a happy workforce at the end of the day. Leaders should be the ones setting the direction and defining the mileposts along the way. Managers can be and should be good leaders focused on short term objectives. This does not excuse them for pushing when they should be pulling, or better yet, marching right along with the employees. All that we mean by true leadership can apply to managers, don't you think?"

I wasn't at all sure. "I don't know. I thought you were going to talk more about mountains then you switched to management.

Do you think leaders are managers first as part of seeing only a mountain or am I mixing too much together and getting a molehill?"

"You're mixing too much together. Let's take me for example. After graduating from college, I worked first as a secretary. There were secretaries in those days, some still taking shorthand. After a while, I became an office manager. As the office manager, my duty, like at your grocery store, was to make sure the work was done. I cared about how people felt, but my focus was on the work. I treated people well because that's the kind of person I was and because I thought it was the right thing to do. I could measure that I was doing well if the daily work was done, everybody went home on time and no one hated my guts.

"I was not really a leader although I led the activities of this small office of clerical people. I think this is the mountain phase of leadership, leading the activities of people.

'Then there is no mountain' happens when you shift from focusing on the work activities or the outcome to the actual people doing the work. This is when leadership becomes confusing and leadership development gets tricky if you ask me."

"I am asking. That's why we're having coffee together. I want to learn from your experience."

"Well, once I got confident running an office, I began to realize the individual needs of the people in the office. All were doing similar, almost identical tasks, but the people were totally different from one another. Over the years I had super-brains to dullards, effervescent people to near zombies. I learned that if I was to get the best out of them, I had to alter my approach to the individuals and teams I was leading. That's when I learned the value of learning. I attended classes and seminars, read books and journals. I think I've subscribed to The Wall Street Journal since the Truman administration.

"This is the tricky part. Some people who take the same road I did, get an education in leadership, apply what they learn to some degree, but don't ever change who they are. They, manager or leader, are stuck in the 'there is no mountain' stage. These are the nominal leaders that we talk about in the collaborative. These people may have the skills, but not the perspective. They don't have the wisdom that true leaders have.

"As I became more experienced as a leader, as I took on more responsibilities for reaching goals, leading larger and larger groups of people, I realized more and more what I didn't know. More classes led to more skills, but no less uncertainty. At that point, I got a coach, which made a tremendous difference. We looked at what I was thinking, what I was feeling, my decisions and the outcomes. We did 360-degree evaluations and included others in monitoring my development. I would tell co-workers that I'm working on such and such a competency and ask them to tell me how I was doing after sixty days."

"That's quite a lot. And risky too."

"That's the whole idea, stretch, but in such a way you can make sense of it. Does no good to try something, fail, and not learn anything."

"Except to say, 'I sure won't do that again.' So, you were in the midst of not seeing the mountain. Have you seen the mountain again?"

Rose smiled. "I hope so. As I said, I got all this training, but still had a sense that it was not enough. I sought mentors and read everything I could about extraordinary leaders. What did they do that I hadn't yet figured out?"

"Business leaders?"

"All kinds of leaders. Jesus as a leader. Mohammed as a leader. The early American presidents and Lincoln, of course. Generals like Patton and emperors like Napoleon. Jack Welch. Henry Ford. Guys like Taiichi Ohno and women like Cary Nation. Other women, too, like Hillary Clinton, Margaret Thatcher and Mother Teresa. I must have studied two or three hundred historic leaders and tried to meet the few contemporary ones that I could. Do you want to know what I learned?"

I nodded encouragement.

"Many of whom we might consider great leaders were not true leaders. They were more like those who see a mountain and push forward. A few were in the middle of no mountain at all. I was intrigued to learn that the famous and very successful University of Alabama football coach, Bear Bryant, said after his retirement that he would have done better by adjusting more to his players' needs than by forcing his own on them. Even he was still seeking to become a true leader. But that's not the most important thing I learned. The significant difference between nominal leaders and true leaders, the difference between no mountain and the second view of the mountain, is getting rid of self-interest. There is no guarantee – but you must lose the 'me.'"

"Catchy."

"Someone like Napoleon was almost totally self-serving. Lincoln, on the other hand, was unusually kind; but he could be equally as merciless to benefit the republic."

"And yet there are ostensibly selfless people doing terrible things in the name of some higher calling," I added.

"That goes back to what Rudy and Bob were talking about, the importance of values, including positive values that support something rather than just be against something. Not easy to do in our world. But I think those three stages of mountain, no mountain, mountain again are a good metaphor for leadership development. Seeing the mountain again requires letting go of the small, personal picture and embracing the greater good."

I told her I agreed with her concept of mountain, no mountain, mountain again and once more asked where she was along the continuum.

"I've certainly given up focusing only on my own good. I've accomplished what I've wanted for my own sense of worth. I have had the good fortune to be professionally successful. Business success, for sure. But I wonder if I've contributed to the greater good. Now I want to learn how I can give back.

"I think I can see the second mountain. It is a bit far away, maybe under some cloud cover, but I know it's there. That feels nice. Can you see the mountain?"

I thought for a moment. "I don't know. I think maybe I have a map that shows where the mountain should be. I'm not sure I can see it in any way but the abstract."

"Maybe we all walk on the mountain for a while before we realize it. Or maybe it is up to others to tell us that we are on it." Rose paused for a moment to sip her coffee. "Here's what I think. Maybe the second mountain isn't a mountain. You know, like 'what is the sound of one hand clapping' or 'what is the sound of rain on a tin roof.'"

"You lost me."

"When you're a true leader, you're no longer a leader in the common sense of what people think a leader is. When you're a true leader, you're in front, you're behind, you're in the middle. The goal is primary, the people are primary, the process is primary. Everything is one thing. You are the mountain, that's why you can't see it. That's what I think."

"Okay, I can fathom that, sort of, maybe."

"Does it make sense? That with leadership, true leadership, the leader is so much a part of the team, the goal, the method, that it all becomes one thing?"

"Yes, it does," I told her, "I want to ponder it for a while. When we get together again, I'll buy the coffee and we can continue this discussion."

"And then maybe we can become the mountain."

6

BUILDING TEAMS

Two of us were scheduled to present during the first hour of the seventh collaborative meeting. For me, it was exhilarating, like preparing to tell my colleagues about my backpacking trip to the top of Mount Whitney.

Three weeks earlier we received assignments that contained a unique task for each of us: Tell two stories. First, a story about a time you tried to perform the assigned task before using the bundled steps we learned in our collaborative. Second, tell a story about using the bundle to perform the task. These before and after stories should take about twenty minutes with the remaining time available for discussion.

My bundle was Building Teams. We had been discussing its components for several weeks. These were the others' assignments.

Harriett	Visioning
Rose	Problem solving
Sid	Delegating
John	Loyalty
Richard	Change
Allen	Communicating
Susan	Learning organization

I wore a sweatshirt for my presentation and had a whistle around my neck. I started my before bundles story by blowing the whistle and shouting, "Listen up. There is no 'I' in TEAM. TEAM means 'Together we Excel And Motivate.'" And then I confessed that this had been about the extent of my before knowledge of building teams.

I knew that everyone on a team needs to participate, have an important role and all that, but I really didn't have a clue about the steps of building a team. What did I know BB? – Before Bundles?

What little I knew came from watching the leaders of teams I had been on, by viewing a few training videos, by reading a few articles about team building and by hiring a couple of consultants to help build teams. I also knew a little from what worked and didn't work when I tried to build them. I explained to the others, without shame, that I really didn't know what I was doing. I was sure my experience was pretty much the same as everyone else's.

After my quick before-bundles presentation, which really wasn't a story of team building at all, as Rudy pointed out, I took off the whistle and the sweatshirt. Underneath was another sweatshirt with printing front and back. On the back, "Lencioni's Dysfunctions." On the front, "Rudy's Four-Part Teaming Model." Everyone laughed.

After the laughter died down, I said with surprising earnestness, "I must tell you, the power of these two models for team building and team maintenance is simply awesome. I proved that to myself in a week.

"With only two items in the team building bundle, you might think it would be easy to try them out. Well, you're right. That's probably why Bob and Rudy chose the teaming bundle to be one of the first. I am truly amazed at how well and how quickly both models worked."

"You mean you didn't think something designed by our very own Rudy would work?" Harriett asked. The group started booing me.

"No, no. That's not it at all." We had become quite a team ourselves. We sometimes laughed like kindergartners.

We had learned that the rationale behind using a leadership bundle is the same as in medicine. Use the entire bundle for best effect; leave out a step and get poorer results. I told the group that I used the Lencioni material first, then Rudy's Four-Part Teaming Model, then Lencioni again. My after story was:

"I met offsite for a couple of hours with my executive team and right off began applying the team-building bundle. First came the Five Dysfunctions survey from Lencioni's book, *The Five Dysfunctions of a Team*. After scoring the surveys, I used a flip chart to explain the five dysfunctions with a particular emphasis on Lencioni's symptoms and unique definitions for each dysfunction.

"I told them that trust means being open and vulnerable with each other. Conflict means engaging in conflict about ideas. Commitments are explicit agreements made by the team. Accountability is peer accountability—peers holding each other accountable for their commitments. Results are team results that every team member works toward; it's about we, not about me.

\	The Five Dysfunctions of a Team	\
Scores	Dysfunctions	Symptoms
7.2	Inattention to Results	Ego and Status
5.9	Avoidance of Accountability	Low Standards
6.8	Lack of Commitment	Ambiguity
6.8	Fear of Conflict	Artificial Harmony
7.3	Absence of Trust	Invulnerability

"Scores under 6 suggest a problem, from 6-7 may be a problem and from 8-9 you're probably doing well. The point of this is to take the waste out of human interactions.

"I started from the bottom, Absence of Trust, and it seemed to make sense to my executive team until I introduced the

Avoidance of Accountability dysfunction with Lencioni's emphasis on "peer" accountability. It was difficult for them to see why they would hold each other accountable given that they were executives responsible for their own departments. Because Fear of Conflict, engaging in ideological conflict, is not one of our team's dysfunctions, we had a lengthy and a bit heated discussion about them already being accountable and not needing ratings from each other. Since this was only an introduction to the model, I told them they could find all the answers in Lencioni's book, and with a little prodding they promised to read it.

"At our next executives' meeting, only three days later, I introduced Rudy's Four-Part Teaming Model which I also sketched out on a flip chart and placed next to the Five Dysfunctions flip chart.

FOUR-PART TEAMING MODEL

Compelling TASK	Sense of MEMBERSHIP
Personal REWARD	INFLUENCE on Team

"I used Rudy's concept of how to introduce a new team member to a team by reintroducing all my executive team members to one another as if they didn't know each other.

"One by one I looked each executive in the eyes and told everyone why he or she was perfectly suited to be on this team.

"There was a hush in the room that we had rarely experienced. Each now knew exactly why he or she belonged and that all the other members of the team knew it, too. When I finished it was clear to all that everyone present had valuable contributions to make. That's how I began the upper right quadrant, the sense of membership, the sense of belonging.

"Then I led a discussion about peer accountability and presented on a flip chart the Basic Agreement that Rudy and Bob used with us in this collaborative.

"We agreed that we would all use it in our future executive team meetings not only to influence the quality of our meetings but to help us work on the peer accountability dysfunction.

> **BASIC AGREEMENT**
> - Show up
> - Participant fully
> - Listen intently
> - Tell the truth
> - Trust the process
> - Honor commitments

"By agreeing to these rules of engagement with one another, we clarified how each of us would influence how the team operated, the influence quadrant of Rudy's model. I made sure during this discussion that all knew how important they are to the team and without their influence, we could not achieve our goals.

"Then we addressed the compelling task quadrant by talking about our work and how important achieving our goals is. Since we previously agreed on compelling goals and our tasks are aligned with these goals, our work is also compelling. Given our relatively high functioning team, I was able to ask some pointed questions. One was, 'Do we all have equally compelling tasks?' The answer was basically yes, different, but all compelling, and each task will contribute in its own way to our success.

"The last thing we discussed was the personal reward quadrant. I asked each of them to tell the group the top three personal rewards that make their work worth doing; that is, after a paycheck. Most of them said the number one reward is the satisfaction of doing good work and being appreciated for that work. Some mentioned feeling like they are an important part of what's going on, knowing the whys and the hows. A few said that our policy of recognizing the importance of our personal lives is a significant payoff.

"I'm amazed that simply discussing the four quadrants with my leadership team boosted our teamwork. A couple of days after the second meeting we met to talk about how well we were doing. They all referred to the Four-Part Teaming Model and how inspiring it is. I can still hear Henry's impassioned statement, 'For the first time in my life, I feel like I am truly a member of a team. I've played on sports teams in high school and college, but now I have a real sense of what being on a team is and how strong a team can be.'"

"Then Mitchell said, 'Just talking about it made a difference in how I respond to you, my teammates. Before, you were just people I worked with. I liked you, but now I appreciate how interdependent we are and that's good. My responsibility is clearer, and I think I like the idea of us being accountable to one another.'"

"Sarah topped it off with, 'I agree completely, and I'm much more interested in investing in becoming a great team, now that we have a clearer idea of what a team is.'"

"I gave them the Lencioni survey again. We were now sevens and eights, in just a few days!"

As I completed my story my colleagues cheered and applauded. What a surprise, and what a great feeling. After the applause subsided, Susan eagerly raised her hand, "May I tell my story?" Bob said, "Absolutely."

"As you all know, I'm primarily a parent; my family is my team. But I'm also a leader of our neighborhood watch. I decided to use the Lencioni model with my watch group. We held the meeting in the daytime when mostly stay-at-home moms get together. There were six of us. I presented the model and asked which dysfunction seemed to be the most difficult for us. It was almost unanimous: lack of trust. I asked each person, in turn, to say what she thought was stopping us from trusting each another. When I got to the third person, she took a deep breath and then blurted, 'I just have to say it. The way Beth treated me last summer at our block party was unforgivable; I can never trust her.'"

"You can imagine what a shock that was to everybody, especially Beth. Bless her, Beth didn't get immediately defensive, but asked what it was she said. To make an intense story short, suffice it to say there was a misunderstanding almost a year ago, festering feelings ever since, and during the meeting a lot of crying and a great catharsis. The model gave us the opportunity to discuss a topic that may never have been opened up otherwise."

Bob chimed in. "That's part of the beauty of the models and of using bundles. They have a solid structure so you know what should be happening and can more easily make it happen."

Sid had a question. "Is there an order to using these two parts of the teaming bundle?"

"Yes, and no," Bob continued. "It depends on the situation and what you want to do. If you have a team that is functioning poorly, I'd start with the Lencioni model. You could give the survey and then discuss what the results mean. At subsequent meetings, you could talk about each of the dysfunctions and decide what changes should be made. If you don't have a damaged team, I'd start with Rudy's Four-Part Teaming Model. I think it's the more powerful and comprehensive way to create and manage a team. You could then use Lencioni to measure progress or to sort out problems as they arise." Bob looked over to Rudy. "What do you think? You created half the teaming bundle."

"I've found all five dysfunctions in Lencioni's work to be very powerful, very useful in any teaming situation. I've also found all four parts the Four-Part Teaming Model to be critical in building high-performing teams. The idea behind a bundle is that you need to use both. So, I would say the question is more about how well you can use them than which one to use first."

The conversation took us over the twenty minutes I had for my report on teaming. I summed up by saying that the two teaming models proved their value and I would forever use them when working with others.

John raised his hand. "Before we move on, I have a question. How do we know how well we're using the bundle? I can see that using either of the teaming models works better than not using them and using both seems like a slam-dunk good idea. I used them last week too, and my scout troop responded very positively. I think, though, that I probably used them differently than others in the collaborative because I'm in a different situation. Is there a standard method or something?"

"I think I can answer that," Susan said. "My bundle is learning organizations and the answer lies in the sophistication of the organization and the idea of mistake-proofing. May I give it a try?"

Rudy and Bob nodded, "Go ahead."

"If you want to create a learning organization you need to

accept, even endorse, the reality of human fallibility. You have to allow people to try something they aren't good at and sometimes make mistakes, even leaders. Then you apply mistake-proofing. Followers who know what to expect can help leaders when the leaders make mistakes. And, if your team knows about the bundled models, they can influence how best to use them. The leader doesn't have to know everything nor do it right every time." Just then Susan noticed Harriett and asked. "You have a question?"

Rudy uncharacteristically interrupted. "Excuse me. Before you ask your question, Harriett, I'd like to remind us that although it is true that we should accept the reality of human fallibility, we also should expect many fewer mistakes when leaders apply bundles rigorously. That is the purpose of bundles. You have a question, Harriett?"

"Actually, less a question than a suggestion. I'm supposed to report on visioning today, but I propose we continue talking about team building and let me report next week. I say that partly because I actually do have a question, partly because there is more to discuss, and partly because I really don't have enough time for my report."

Richard polled the group. "Thumbs?" Everyone around the table held a thumb pointing up. Since none pointed down, Harriet's proposal was accepted. Early in the collaborative, Bob and Rudy introduced this Thumb Method of decision-making, and we've continued to use it whenever a team decision is needed. It works like this: After sufficient discussion, someone makes a proposal. We all indicate our level of support for the proposal by pointing a thumb up, sideways, or down. Up means, "I really like this proposal and you can count on me 100% to do my part." Sideways means, "I have concerns, maybe even doubts, but you can count on me 100% to do my part." Down means, "I'm not doing it; my concerns are just too great." It's amazing how this simple visible procedure reduces ambiguity and overcomes some of Lencioni's lack of commitment dysfunction.

"Great," Harriet said. "I guess my question has to do with the psychology of a team. Or maybe it's the difference between a team and a group. A good team has an overriding goal, more important than individual goals. I wonder about the value of a team versus the value of a highly functional workgroup like ours. We're sort of a working group and that's fine. We don't have an overriding mutual goal; it's more like we're here for our own benefit and for the company we work for."

"So," Bob answered, "you're wondering about the value of creating a team, the effort involved, that sort of thing, and the relative payoff. Is that it?"

"Yes."

Rudy looked at me. "Let's ask our expert, the guy giving us his excellent report."

I was up to the challenge. "When we look at Lencioni's model," I said, "notice that absence of trust, the inability to be vulnerable with each other, is the foundational dysfunction. I think that's a huge difference between a working group and a team. On a team, you continually increase trust in one another by being vulnerable during all aspects of the model, from 'trust' to 'paying attention to results.' A group is made up of individuals with varied commitment to the outcome and certainly to each other. It seems to me that any effort to build a team gives you results far superior to simply gathering together a workgroup. And my guess is that anyone who has been on a great team will always want to be on another, not on just a working group."

"That's exactly right," Rudy said. "The reason to do an entire team bundle, rather than just selected parts, is to maximize the probability that you'll transform a group into a fully functioning team that gets superior results. Use the entire team building bundle, both models, get feedback from participants, and continually get better."

We discussed Rudy's point for a while. Bundles make so much sense. An electrical system is made up of bundles. Leave one out and the system doesn't work. People are complicated. Leave out something subtle but important, and people can get hurt, discouraged, angry, even quit if the omission is important enough. With bundles, you can knowingly apply the best thinking toward achieving a very clear target. If it isn't working, you have a finite list of things to analyze and fix.

Before we finished, I gave everyone two handouts:

> **Making the Building Teams bundle work**
>
> - Agree on a compelling TASK, nothing trivial
> - Agree on team MEMBERSHIP, why every member is exactly the right person
> - Agree on how team members will INFLUENCE decisions about how the team will work to accomplish the compelling task
> - Identify significant personal REWARDS that each team member will get from working to accomplish the compelling task

The first summarizes the Four-Part Teaming Model and the second the Five Dysfunctions of a Team.

> **And while doing that...**
>
> - Demonstrate TRUST by becoming more vulnerable with the team
> - Engage in significant ideological CONFLICT that dispels artificial harmony
> - Make each COMMITMENT explicit and visible to reduce ambiguity
> - Hold each other ACCOUNTABLE for fulfilling our commitments so our standards don't slip
> - Pay more attention to our agreed upon TEAM RESULTS than to our egos or status.

I think the team building bundle was a great bundle to start with. You can't get better than that. Lencioni's dysfunctions rock. Rudy's Four-Part Teaming Model rocks. Bundles rock.

7

A TEAM WITH A VISION

Bob began the next collaborative session with, "All the highest functioning teams have a vision, an inspiring purpose, to strive toward. Once you have a compelling vision you can apply the Four-Part Teaming Model to ground your team and Lencioni's Five Dysfunctions to polish its functioning. Without a compelling vision, no task the team takes on will be compelling enough to produce the highest level of team functioning. Without a compelling vision, you may as well clean out your desk and go home."

Which brought us to Harriett's visioning presentation. Harriett started with, "So many vision statements from well-known companies are surprisingly flat, merely chains of clichés like, 'Be the best…, the industry leader in…, bring innovation to…' Others are delightful, like Disney's, 'To make people happy.' Then there is

Honda's more aggressive, 'We will crush, squash, and slaughter Yamaha.' Here are some others I like.

- Wal-Mart, 'To give ordinary folk the chance to buy the same thing as rich people.'
- Mary Kay Cosmetics, 'To give unlimited opportunity to women.'
- The 3M Company, 'To solve unsolved problems innovatively.'
- Merck, 'To preserve and improve human life.'

"You'll notice that the best visions don't mention products, but what products can accomplish. A vision is a collective dream that can and must be accomplished. Ideally, you want a vision that tugs on emotions, heats the blood, and drives you to move a mountain rock by rock with your bare hands, if necessary, to reach your goal. It inspires individual workers and the organization to accomplish great things."

I'd heard that before. What was different and what resonated with me was when she said, "If an employee doesn't know the company vision you have a worker; if an employee knows the company vision you have a contributor; if the employee believes in the company vision you have a partner."

Harriett continued, "The key to understanding the

importance of a vision is to realize that people do only what they consciously or unconsciously value. Value always starts with, 'What's in it for me?' The task is to align the 'What's in it for me,' with a vision statement. Want to see how that works?"

We all agreed. This is where it got very interesting.

"Right now," Harriett said, "we're a bunch of individuals working on reaching individual goals. We're doing it together, as a working group, but we're not really a team striving toward some grand vision. Agree?"

We all agreed again.

"Then let's form a high functioning team. Now, today, in the next sixty minutes." She looked over to Bob and Rudy. "Do you guys agree?"

"Sure. Have at it."

"Want us to help?"

"Yes," Harriett answered. "Why don't you start by pretending that this group of individuals is meeting for the first time and you want to form a team: What would you do?"

Rudy started. "We've brought you together for a very compelling purpose. Today, more than ever before, the world needs good leadership. With a global economy, increasing energy costs, dwindling resources, higher customer expectations, greater competition, I could go on and on, but the point is the stakes are high. The bottom line is that business mistakes are costly. Leaders must bring skills to the marketplace that avoid these mistakes. You have been brought together to begin the important process of mistake-proofing you as leaders."

Bob stood up, walked around the table and stood behind Richard. "We asked Richard to join us in this effort because of his extensive military experience. He has led soldiers into the most trying conditions imaginable and brings us the leadership perspective that can be gained only in life or death situations."

Bob went to Allen sitting to Richard's right. He put one hand on Allen's shoulder. "Allen is a farmer. No one can have the breadth of practical applied cyclical experience as a farmer. He has the challenge of creating a new team with almost every harvest. It is important to our mix to have Allen with us."

Next, Bob went to Susan. "You might wonder why we wanted a homemaker on our team. Our stay-at-home Mom is uniquely qualified to know why we lead the way we do. Her values drive what she does. Home and hearth. Family and relationships. Susan brings relational perspective to our group."

I was next. I could feel his hands on my shoulders. "This guy is probably our most 'with-it' member. He probably knows how to set the blinking clock on a DVD player. His knowledge of marketing and matching inventory to ever-changing demand is critical in today's business climate and we know he has great insights to share."

He went to Rose. "One word for Rose, 'wisdom.' She has forgotten more than anyone of us has learned. All we have to do is ask and she will provide."

Now Sid. "This man is probably the most traveled and has lived in more countries than any of us including the Colonel. We wanted someone who had a greater world perspective to share ideas and perspective that may be foreign, but foreign only because of unfamiliarity, not value."

Next was John. "If anyone ever needs to understand the value of a moral compass, this experienced scout leader can give you a hundred reasons, all of them maturing young men. John brings the perspective of investing in the future."

He ended standing behind Harriett. "And we have the benefit of a politician. What a great person to have on our team. She is someone who knows the inner workings of our government, how to make seemingly impossible things happen, and how to avoid the huge disasters that can occur if we're not vigilant."

Bob concluded by saying, "You all have much to contribute beyond my few sentences. Each of you was deliberately chosen from the many that applied for this particular collaborative. We wanted to create a team, not just a working group."

"I get it," Allen said. "This is part of the 'Membership' quadrant of the four-part model and the mistake-proofing ourselves as leaders is the 'Task' quadrant."

"Very good," Rudy replied. "As Harriett suggested, we're going to form a team today. How better than to start with our teaming bundle?"

Harriett stood up. "Now we're going to do the other two quadrants: influence on the team and personal reward. We're going to do both of them at the same time by creating a vision for our collaborative team that will make our task of learning to mistake-proof our leadership even more compelling. We'll do it together so each of us can influence what the vision says and what it means. And our vision will be rewarding to each of us."

Harriett moved to the front wall and unfastened three rolled-up flip charts, each starting with "It is now 15 years in the future when you have achieved your most cherished desires with respect to this collaborative team and its impact." Each flip chart also had one of the following three statements:

- In this future, what do you want people in your company to say about you?

- In this future, what do you want this collaborative team to say about you?

- In this future, what do you want our nation to say about you?

We divided into dyads and began writing words and phrases on sticky notes that we thought would best answer each of the three questions. I worked with John and we came up with things like high functioning, well respected, profitable, industry leader, innovative, fast-growing, envied by all, value, community leader, and a few others, some very compelling, at least for us.

Each pair posted their sticky notes on the appropriate flip chart, and then we devoted a few minutes to reading all of them. It wasn't clear yet, but I believed that a vision just might emerge from the integration of these ideas.

Harriett plowed on by having us multi-vote the words and phrases on the charts. Everyone was given ten red dots and told to put a dot next to words or phrases that were particularly compelling to us individually, but no one could put more than one dot per word or phrase. The five phrases with the most dots were:

> Vision concepts/words
>
> Great outcomes
> Highest functioning
> Inspired true leadership
> Using bundles
> Mistake-proofed

We then re-formed into our small groups with the task to create a fifteen word or shorter vision statement using these five phrases and whatever was on one of the three flip charts she assigned to us. We had ten minutes. Each group put their statement on a flip chart and we multi-voted for two. Ours wasn't one of the two.

> This team will revolutionize leadership and reinvent how businesses succeed.

> We will contribute to our community in ways that can't currently be imagined.

John and I thought it was a little unfair that neither winning entry used any of the five phrases all of us had identified, but we admitted that the statements were a whole lot better than the pathetic effort we came up with.

We then discussed what we liked about each one, what was weak, and what concepts were missing that should be there. Harriet listed our ideas on a whiteboard.

We toyed with different combinations. Then voted on phrases, tried some more, voted some more. Finally, we came up with a statement that everyone liked.

> **Our Vision**
>
> We will release the power of leadership bundles on the world.

I liked our statement. It made me feel good.

"So, are we a team?" Rudy asked.

We nodded our heads and pretty much agreed we were a

team. Not the highest functioning team yet—that would come only with further application of the teaming bundle—but still a team and not just a group. I spoke up, "I don't think we would have said that before we created our vision statement."

Sid raised his hand and asked, "I agree that it feels like we have more of a team now. Two hours ago, I would have said we were a group. What do you think made such a difference?"

"That's my point," Harriett said. "Our vision statement is inspiring to each of us. Before we created it, we agreed to work hard on mistake-proofing our leadership, but as individuals. Our mutual vision makes mistake-proofing even more compelling."

Rudy interjected, "That's true, but think of the team building bundle. Think Lencioni for a minute. We now have a clear result we can pay attention to. We trusted each other enough to engage in robust ideological conflict as we polished our vision. We are beginning to make more solid commitments to each other. And as we continue in this collaborative, we are more likely to hold each other accountable to help achieve our vision. I believe that as we intentionally work on overcoming each of the five dysfunctions, we will not only feel that we are a team, as some of you have suggested, we will prove it.

"We also used the Four-Part Teaming Model to deal with our collective need to work on something compelling, to feel that we each belong, to know that we do have influence on this team, and to identify the significant personal reward defined in our vision."

"So, campers," Bob said, "the leadership team building bundle is Rudy's Four-Part Teaming Model, Lencioni's Five Dysfunctions *and* visioning. As we said earlier, a good approach is to introduce Rudy's model at the start, especially being very clear why each member belongs on the team. Another way to use it is to put the model on a board and have people write on it what their individual payoffs are, what influence they want to have on the team, why they belong and what the team's compelling task is.

You can have them take the Lencioni survey found in his *The Five-Dysfunctions of a Team,* talk together about what the scores mean, and construct a plan to raise the scores. And, last, but not least as we have seen, use the power of an emotionally compelling vision to define a future that team members will strive together to accomplish."

After a few more comments from team members, Harriett concluded her presentation with, "What's amazing is that for high functioning teams, a mutual vision, Rudy's compelling task, and Lencioni's team results are inextricably joined."

I think everyone was feeling the same sense of near euphoria that I was feeling.

Too soon, Sid broke the moment, "I have a question. Is there just one vision for the entire organization?"

Susan said she'd like to try an answer. "Yes and no. The typical answer is that the organization needs a compelling vision to inspire and set direction, but that individual units within the organization also need a vision more specific to their work to motivate smaller teams. And some say that each worker should have a personal vision. Obviously, the individual and unit visions should support the larger vision.

"I say that one vision is enough—if it resonates with everyone's personal values. The problem is that words are ambiguous, and people are complex. An inspiring vision for one person can be meaningless to another. Take our vision. We all feel really good about 'unleashing leadership bundles.' And it further explains our task of mistake-proofing our leadership. But I know that lots of people won't be inspired by either our vision or our task.

"Somehow each team member must be captured by an inspiring vision from their organization, their department or the creative juices of their team. If none of these are forthcoming, the person left with only a personal vision will not thrive on that team."

"Excellent, Susan, excellent," Rudy said. "That's why for a team to function at its best, it must have a vision that resonates with the values of each individual.

"To sum up, for a team to function at its best, it must reap the benefits of the Four-Part Teaming Model, Lencioni's Five Dysfunctions, and a compelling vision. That's our complete teaming bundle."

And that was the end of that day's collaborative.

On the drive home I thought it was fascinating how we had

morphed the definition of the team building bundle from Lencioni and the Four-Part Teaming Model to now include visioning. It definitely was more powerful. I had earlier toyed with including the Basic Agreement (show up, participate fully, listen intently, tell the truth, trust the process, and honor commitments) in the bundle, but hadn't mentioned it.

8

HARNESSING THE SPEED OF THOUGHT

Today's collaborative was billed as, "How to solve every problem, resolve every conflict and live a happy and successful life." I had learned not to doubt the two guys, but this was stretching it.

Bob started his part of the presentation by announcing the title and asking if anyone believed that a leadership bundle could do such a thing. I raised my hand to agree that it could, but no one else did. "Okay, team," I asked, "Why doesn't anyone else agree with me—and Bob and Rudy?"

"First of all," Rose said, "not all problems can be solved."

"And not all conflicts can be resolved," added Sid.

"Happiness is transient." This from John the Scout leader.

"How can one bundle do all that?" Allen wanted to know.

Maybe my faith was misplaced.

Rudy to the rescue. "Today you will learn how to solve every problem and resolve every conflict and you can use this ability to then live a happy and successful life. With this disclaimer."

A bunch of guffaws were heard from the peanut gallery.

"Wait," Rudy said, "before you pass judgment. The disclaimer is simply that this bundle can help solve any problem that can be solved, let you know very early on when the problem cannot be solved, and help you divide an unsolvable problem into smaller problems that can be solved. The same is true for conflicts. I predict that you will be so impressed that once you become expert with this bundle, you will proclaim this same now scoffed at description when you teach others this bundle. Is that good enough for you naysayers?"

They all agreed.

"By the way," Rudy added. "This next bundle is Bob's creation."

John held up his cup of coffee. "I sure hope Bob's creation is as good as this coffee. It's terrific."

Our setting was terrific too. We had ensconced ourselves around Susan's home dining room table for our collaborative meeting. I'm sure it must have been hard for her, following Bob and Rudy's "distraction avoidance rule" by providing only liquid refreshment: coffee, tea, juice and water. But it was great coffee and great juice.

"All right, campers," Bob said, getting up. "Here's the deal." He walked around the table handing out fake ten thousand-dollar bills. "I'm giving you each ten thousand dollars…"

"If it's fake money why don't you make it a million dollars?" I don't know why I say things like that, but I do. Bob continued.

"Pretend the money is real and it is to be used for all of you to take a week's vacation together. The only stipulation is that each day you must spend at least eight waking hours together."

"What about our families?"

"Along with our ability to give out tens of thousands of dollars, we can suspend the laws of time and space. You'll experience a week's vacation. Your family won't even notice you're gone. So, don't worry about them. What I want you to do for the next ten minutes or so is decide on the vacation you'll take together. Understand?"

We all said yes.

Susan started us off. "With ten thousand dollars, we could go a lot of places. I vote for Tuscany."

"I like Tuscany. We could also go to Paris." Sid's thought sounded good. Then ideas began to fly.

"A cruise among the Greek islands."

"Alaska."

"New Zealand and the Cook Glacier."

"Mountain climbing lessons."

"Scuba diving in Belize."

"You can use the flip chart," Rudy suggested. They had brought a portable one that stood just outside the dining area. So we did. Within two minutes, we had listed twenty-six ideas. Then we started debating the pros and cons of each. It seemed like for every pro someone had a con. After five more minutes, we had culled only five ideas from our list.

"Okay, stop there," Bob instructed. "You all fell into the speed of thought trap."

"You mean we don't get to go on vacation?" Rose sounded genuinely sad.

"Not today. What's the first thing you did once I gave you the money and asked you to plan your vacation together?"

We all looked at one another. What was the first thing we did?

Susan raised her hand. "I think I suggested Tuscany."

Sid nodded. "Then I added Paris."

"That's right," Bob said. He went over to the flip chart and tore off our list of possibilities. "You listed places you could go, then debated about which one would be the best. Is that right?"

We all agreed.

"Classic mistake. I gave you a problem and you started discussing the solution. Sounds logical. Rarely works. But we approach problems the same way, all day, every day. That, teammates, is a common invisible business disaster."

Richard began shaking his head. "Bob, you're going to have to explain that one."

Bob bowed. "It will be my pleasure.

"Whenever you face a problem, an issue, an opportunity, use five steps to solve it. Not three. Not four. All five. That's the bundle. You didn't do that. Instead, you used three steps: step one, the opportunity, step four, possible solutions, and a pathetic version of step five, debate solutions until one wins.

"I gave you step one when I gave you the money and the challenge of deciding on a vacation. Often in life, the issue to be addressed is not that clear, but I simplified it for you and you still messed up."

We booed, but, as usual, he ignored us and continued as if nothing had happened.

"I'm not going to dwell on what you missed, but what you did. Let's say you eventually decide that the best solution is to go with the first idea, Tuscany." Bob went to the flip chart and wrote:

> 1. Issue, problem, opportunity: *Spend a week's vacation with one another.*
>
> 2.
>
> 3.
>
> 4. List possible solutions
>
> 5. Best solution: *Go to Tuscany.*

"You have step one, four and five. Any idea what the other steps are?" He didn't wait for an answer. "Of course, you don't.

But do you see that you went from step one to step four, ignoring other steps that might be important?"

"We considered that, but we were in a hurry to go on vacation," Harriet said.

Bob narrowed his eyes. "Right. Do you want to guess what they are, or shall I just tell you?"

"Tell us." Bob filled in the other two:

> 1. Issue, problem, opportunity: *Spend a week's vacation with one another.*
>
> 2. Define the goal
>
> 3. List hurdles and concerns
>
> 4. List possible solutions
>
> 5. Best solution: *Go to Tuscany.*

"Does this make logical sense?"

"It makes logical sense, but isn't the goal going to Tuscany?" Allen asked.

Bob smiled and pointed his finger at Allen. "No. Tuscany is the solution. You guys never defined the goal. I repeat you came up with a solution to reach a goal no one agreed to because it was never defined."

"Keep talking."

"I gave you the problem or actually the opportunity of

spending a week's vacation together. That's step one. Step two is defining what your goal is. What is a vacation? Relaxation? A time to travel? A time to learn something? Explore? Have an adventure? Meet new people? A vacation can be a lot of things. As teams or individuals, once we identify a problem our minds rush to solutions without careful consideration of what we truly want to accomplish. Put two people together to plan a vacation and you better make sure both have the same idea in mind."

"You got that right," Richard said. "I don't know how long it took me to learn that my idea of a vacation at a seaside golf course did not mesh with my wife's idea of a vacation at a mountain lake."

"So," Rudy asked, "What is your definition of a vacation?" The answers we gave ranged from total relaxation to heart-pumping daredevil stunts. "You can see," he said, "that you might have debated long and hard about which vacation was the best one because you had a lot of different definitions and those differences were totally unknown. That's why you must define the goal as the second step before you go looking for solutions. Do that by listing all your definitions and agreeing on which one or combination meets the needs of everyone. You might agree that the characteristics of the ideal group vacation include travel to a foreign country, great food, equal parts relaxation and activities, and maybe somewhere that is dry and warm."

That made great sense to me, but I needed some clarification. "Then," I asked, "we compare our list of possible real solutions to our list of abstract concepts?"

"We'll do that, but not quite yet; first we need one more element, step three. Once you define the goal in measurable terms, so you know how to judge possible solutions and know when you've reached the goal, you list everything you can think of that may be an obstacle to reaching the goal. For example, let's say one of you is afraid to fly. That might restrict how far you can travel or require you to find a way around that hurdle, like learning not to be afraid or getting medicine to help overcome the fear. Here is the complete 'Harnessing the Speed of Thought' bundle.

> Harnessing the Speed of Thought
>
> 1. Identify the issue, problem or opportunity
> 2. Define the goal
> 3. List hurdles/concerns
> 4. List possible solutions
> 5. Choose the best solution

"Like all bundles, you must do all the steps. Most people skip two and three and waste a lot of time and energy on four and five. Think of the last committee meeting you attended. I'll bet it was just like what you did with the vacation exercise, list possible solutions and debate their relative merits, oblivious to the reality that everyone there saw the situation differently."

"A very interesting idea," Rose said. "How and when would you use it?"

"When to use it is all the time," Bob answered. "How to use it is always sequential: understand what the issue is, define the goal, list the hurdles and think of all the possible solutions you can before trying to decide on a best solution. Imagine someone comes to you and says, 'We should raise the price point for our luxury widget.' That's a solution so you should ask, 'What is the problem you're addressing?' The answer might be, 'We need to improve our bottom line.' But that is a solution too. When a sentence has the word 'need' in it, it is usually a solution disguised as a problem. So you might ask that person, 'Why do we need to improve our bottom line?' And the answer might be, 'Because the board has indicated that our new management system must show results this year or heads will roll.' So the real problem is board dissatisfaction. Should that problem be addressed by increasing the price of the product?

"Carry this model around in your mind. Use it to create a meeting agenda. Apply it to any problem. The bundle requires that either you start with step one, or you get others who have already raced to step four to come back to step one. People hate coming back. At first, you'll sound like Johnny-one-note always asking, 'What is the issue?' But once people experience its value, it becomes almost automatic.

"There are two rules of thumb when you use Harnessing the Speed of Thought.

"Rule 1: mutually agree on each step before you move to the next step. If you can't agree, then either divide the problem into smaller units or agree that you can't solve this one to everyone's satisfaction.

"Rule 2: the 4-3-2-1 rule. This means that in practice about forty percent of time and effort will be spent on identifying and agreeing on the issue. Thirty percent will be spent on defining a mutual goal. Twenty percent will be on identifying hurdles and only ten percent on listing solutions and agreeing on the best one. Of course, implementation of complex solutions may take a long time and a few more visits to each step."

The room was quiet as we absorbed this information. John broke the silence. "I get it. You hyped this bundle as solving every problem and resolving every conflict because conflicts occur when people race to solutions and argue about which solution is best. This method avoids that argument by having everyone agree to the goal, which makes mutually selecting the best solution much easier. Brilliant!"

Bob bowed. "Thank you."

"Do you want to know what your homework is?" Rudy asked,

We all booed again.

He continued. "It's for your own good. At the next meeting you attend, any place where people are sorting something out, notice if they assemble solutions using our five steps or if they swirl around. Then make a promise to yourself to never swirl again. Try Harnessing the Speed of Thought in your own meetings. Then practice, practice, practice. And come back and tell us about it."

"That's it?"

"That's it. We're done for today."

* * *

Over the next couple of days, I observed groups working together. They swirled. I mean they really swirled. Made me dizzy. The handouts we received on this bundle helped me understand why people race to solutions; it has to do with the brain, evolution, improving survival probabilities and the like.

The story I'm going to tell at the next collaborative will be about how I used the tool to have a successful conversation with an important customer. Once we decided what the issue was, we focused on defining the goals she wanted to achieve and the hurdles that might get in the way. She thought that was great because it was mostly about her and her company's desires. After we listed a few potential solutions, I realized with just a bit of tweaking we could make a mutually advantageous deal. And we did. It was that simple. I was beginning to love bundles.

9

DELEGATING

A major tenet of our collaborative is that if you are to mistake-proof leadership, you must do the things that really ought to be done and do them well. That's true with delegating. Take the time to do it right and there is a very high probability that the results will be right, especially when the difference between delegator and delegatee are hierarchical.

On the other hand, the more the two are collegial the more they tend to make assumptions and race to conclusions that won't match. Best to do every step, every time, really well.

At our next collaborative, we learned the delegation bundle. It's one of the easiest to apply and is about as logical as a management bundle can be.

Rudy wrote on the whiteboard...

> **Stephen R. Covey's Delegation Model**
> 1. Desired result
> 2. Guidelines
> 3. Resources
> 4. Accountability
> 5. Consequences

I was inspired by Rudy's recitation of Covey's story of delegating important yard work to his youngest son. As homage to his delightful story, this is what happened the first time I used the model.

I wanted our son Zack to clean the garage. My father would have told me, "I want the garage cleaned by Saturday afternoon. Make sure you do it right," and that would have been it. Invariably, I wouldn't do it right and have to spend another hour or two on the project. And, truth be told, that's pretty much how I usually delegated to Zack

Zack is nine years old. He's a typical fourth grader: kinda likes girls, but doesn't admit it, loves baseball, hates chores, and forgets everything you tell him within three minutes. Delegating anything to him almost always results in somebody being angry, somebody being hurt, and somebody being frustrated, usually me, him, and my wife, in that order.

This is my delegation conversation with Zack after Bob and Rudy explained Covey's model.

"Hi, Zack. I have some work for you to do today."

"Aw, Dad. I want to play baseball this morning. It's Saturday. I'm a kid. I should be outdoors playing."

"I agree and I want you to do that, as soon as you get some important work done."

"Sounds like a chore to me."

"This is the deal. The garage is a mess. Mostly with your stuff."

"I don't think it's a mess."

"Would you agree it's a mess if I can't get the car in the garage, I can't find tools when I need them, and even you have trouble finding your stuff?"

He shrugged his shoulders. "Maybe."

"Would you agree it's more a minor problem than a major problem?"

"Yes," he agreed immediately, probably thinking it would be a quick chore.

"Me, too. Here's what I want: The garage clear enough so I can get the car in and me out of the car without the car or any door hitting anything.'

"That's it?" Zack asked, an astonished look on his face.

"Just a bit more." He kept his optimistic look. "I want all the tools on the workbench put away in the right places, so the workbench has absolutely nothing on it. And, I want all of your stuff back in your bin where it belongs."

"Okay."

"And I'll be in the living room if you have any questions, so you don't have to guess about where to put anything."

"Okay."

"I'd like it done before noon. And if you want, you can promise your brother a dollar if you get him to help you. I'll provide the dollar."

"How much do I get?"

"This will count as a chore toward your allowance. But if you get done before eleven and pass inspection, I'll add another couple of dollars toward your new catcher's mitt. If you don't get done by noon, I'll expect you to keep at it until you do pass inspection. Deal?"

"Deal."

By ten-thirty, he was back in the living room asking for his work to be inspected. That was too quick I thought but followed him into the garage. There was space for the car and the car doors to open. The workbench was completely cleared off and every tool was in the proper place. None of his stuff was to be seen.

I was astonished that he was able to get the job done. I asked him how he did it. He looked at me with an expression only a nine-year-old could pull off and said, "Dad, it was because I knew what to do."

Such a simple yet profound concept made difficult in the business world because leaders don't attend to the importance of both getting the work done and growing the people. It's the classic struggle defining what we need to do and organizing how the work gets done. Good delegating bridges this gap between what and how.

Maybe twenty years ago I asked an employee to deliver some supplies to a store about forty miles away. Our truck was on its last legs, so I cautioned him to make sure there was plenty of radiator fluid and gas before he left. Which he did. I didn't tell him to check the oil. Evidently, he didn't, even though he was under the hood checking the radiator. You can guess what happened. Oil had been leaking, hardly any left, engine burned up. My guess is that he figured that since I always told him what to do, if I didn't tell him about the oil, he didn't have to do it. I was ignorant of my role in the failure until Covey.

A good example of delegating happened just last week. We were contacted by a new, potentially very important customer. I decided to let my right-hand man, actually, a woman, Phyllis, handle this opportunity from start to finish. I had Covey's items written out and simply went down the list.

"Phyllis," I said, "I want to delegate Mr. Wood's call to you."

She smiled. "And use Covey's model to do it?"

"Yes. There are four desired results: First, Mr. Wood understands what we can do for him; second, we understand what he needs from us; third, he knows that we understand his needs; and fourth, he makes a decision to buy, in that order."

Phyllis saluted. "Got it, boss. How about guidelines?"

"You know our values. No matter what the outcome, I want Mr. Wood to be happy with the process and more knowledgeable about us after than before. If he doesn't buy now, he may buy later. His friends may buy later, too."

"And what kind of resources can I have?"

"Ten percent of your time can be spent making this happen. You decide what kind of budget you want to spend. I will be available for help if you need it."

"Next?"

"As for boundaries, I think Mr. Wood should make a decision by the middle of next month, so do what you feel necessary to make that happen before then."

"What's in it for me, boss?"

"Ah, consequences," I said. "Do this one well and you get five percent of the account for the first two years. But you knew that. In addition, this will mark one more step in your advancement to running the show when I'm old and grey. If it doesn't work, then you and I will sit down and learn at least two things. Agreed?"

"Agreed."

I see delegating as a blueprint. It's so obvious. You use a blueprint to build something as logical as a house. Why not use a blueprint to construct something as nebulous as a conversation between two people?

The guys also had put something else on a flip chart:

> 1. **Wait** – I'll let you know when it's time to act.
>
> 2. **Ask** – Inquire if you think something should be done.
>
> 3. **Recommend** – When you have an idea you want to implement.
>
> 4. **Do it and report immediately** – So I can check it.
>
> 5. **Do it and report routinely** – At your convenience

This is also from Covey. How you want the delegatee to follow-up with you should also be defined in one of several ways: Don't do a thing until I tell you. Check with me before you act. Ask me when you think action should be taken. Let me know right away when the deed is done or let me know at your convenience when you're finished. It's part of setting boundaries during delegation.

Phyllis continued, "How do you want me to report back to you?"

"You tell me. How much rope do you want?"

"I'm pretty confident. Why don't I get back to you after he makes his decision?"

"That much?"

"Yep."

"Have fun."

And I meant it. No worries.

Early in my career, prior to Covey, I was probably like everyone else, caught between not having the time to do the job myself and blending inadequate delegation with way too much micro-managing. This model helps me delegate quickly and effectively. I win. My staff wins. My customers win. There is a trend to this bundling business.

10

CUSTOMER AND EMPLOYEE LOYALTY

I hate role-playing. Most people hate role-playing. Naturally, the guys had us role-playing. But before we role played, we talked loyalty. Customer loyalty. Employee loyalty. Family loyalty. Loyalty oaths. Loyalty cards. Loyalty days. Loyal opposition. I didn't know loyalty had so many permutations.

Rudy presented some interesting facts. "Research on web-based businesses found that loyalty in e-commerce is dismal. Of 1,000 visitors to a website, only about 18 purchase anything. Of that 18, only two purchase again. People come and go at the click of a mouse. Attention spans are lightning quick. Gratification in cyberspace is almost instantaneous. Another opportunity to buy is as close as Google.

"Potential customers of brick and mortar places like hairdressers, physicians, auto repair shops, and so on aren't much better. No one returns to a doctor they don't think is competent, and few return to a barber after a hair disaster. That is unless the business uses the loyalty bundle. Our objective today is to learn how to create and sustain loyalty in customers and employees. Bob will introduce the first half of our loyalty bundle."

"We start with the Four Cs," Bob said writing on a flip chart.

> The Four Cs
>
> 1. Connect – human to human
> 2. Collaborate – form a partnership
> 3. Contribute – service, information, respect
> 4. Confirm – nothing was missed

After briefly explaining each of the Four Cs, Bob declared, "No matter what the situation, if you do the four Cs, all of them, good things will happen. Now, let's get on with the role play." Everyone groaned.

I was playing a store clerk of some undetermined kind. Rose played a customer and Sid was my coach to help out when I floundered. I was to do the Four Cs as well as I could. Rose was to do whatever was written on a 3 X 5 card Bob gave her.

First off, I wanted to connect human-to-human, the first C in the bundle.

I looked Rose in the eyes and in my most friendly voice and with an engaging smile said, "Good morning Ma'am. How may I be of service?"

"I'm looking for a…"

Sid interrupted looking at me with feigned disgust. "That sounded so fake."

"I'm supposed to be connecting."

"Be yourself. That's who should connect. Not some game show host."

"Point taken." In a normal tone, I said the same thing again. Rose started again.

"I'm looking for a tree I can plant in my backyard: something that will provide shade but will not grow too tall." Evidently, I was working in some sort of plant store or nursery.

"I can help you with that." I figured if I just kept being my naturally friendly self, I would keep connecting. Anyway, the team would give me feedback later. I was soon off to collaborate, the second C. "Did you have anything particular in mind?"

"No. I know so little about trees and plants."

"Would it help if I showed you trees that provide both good shade and don't grow much, so you can get an idea of what's available?" Sid nodded his head and pointed his finger at me, then did the "okay" sign.

Rose and I talked more so I could learn exactly what she wanted. I thought we did the collaborative bit quite well. What helped me most was thinking that I truly wanted to partner with her in solving her problem. Then on to the third C, contribute, making up everything as I went along because I don't know trees.

"I'm pretty sure I know what you're looking for and you have three good choices; the pigmy Japanese Maple, the dwarf Hemlock, and the Junior Oak. Let me show you examples of each, and we can talk about their individual advantages and disadvantages."

"Oh, that would be grand," Rose said clapping her hands and tilting her head in awe.

"Significantly overacted," Sid said, "but good."

I showed Rose three imaginary trees and began describing as many of their features as I could think of. Then, I remembered with confirming, the fourth C, I want to give my customer every chance to express dissatisfaction. I said to Rose, "Which of these will work best for you? Or if you don't like any of them, we can look for others you might like better and figure out how to make them work."

"You know," she said, "You may be right. I don't like any of these."

Bob cut in, "How was that, team?"

"I thought it was well done," Rose said. "I felt he cared about me and what I wanted. He connected human-to-human throughout, he collaborated with me to find out exactly what I wanted, he contributed his," she laughed, "seemingly endless knowledge about trees, and his effort to let me express dissatisfaction with his tree options while attempting to confirm my satisfaction, letting me say what I really wanted to say."

Others made equally flattering comments until Allen suggested that my boss would have been angry that I let my customer get away. And if on commission, I didn't get paid.

Rose jumped back in with, "Better to uncover the dissatisfaction now than after the expense of buying, transporting and planting the tree. And the bad-mouthing you would get every time I looked at the tree for the next 30 years."

It was time to move on to the second half of the loyalty bundle. Rudy explained that this part came from Development Dimensions International, DDI for short, a comprehensive provider of leadership and human resources materials. "It's called 'Take the H.E.A.T,' and has four steps a person should take when an interaction goes wrong." He wrote on the flip chart:

Take the H.E.A.T.

- **H** Hear them out
- **E** Empathize
- **A** Apologize
- **T** Take responsibility for action

Like with the Four Cs, Rudy gave minimal explanation and then said, "It's time for our next role play." I expected groans, but they didn't come. I guess we learned from the first one that role plays work pretty well.

John became the customer with a new 3 X 5 card. Allen the

employee and Susan the coach.

"Good morning, sir; how may I be of service?" Allen didn't make the same mistake I did. He sounded friendly but normal.

"It's not a good morning at all. You people screwed up. I want my money back!"

The team roared. Scout leader John was way out of character. His face was red, and his voice was dripping with venom.

"Ahhh," was all Allen could say.

Susan offered some coaching. "Ask him what happened."

"What happened?"

"I rented a car from you this morning. I got no more than out of the city and into the middle of nowhere when the engine died and wouldn't start again. It took me two hours to get hold of somebody and at least another hour to get back to civilization."

Allen threw up his hands. "Hey, take it easy; I didn't do it."

Susan immediately jumped on that one, "Hear him out. Don't interrupt."

"Okay, please continue sir."

"I didn't get to my appointment and wasted an entire workday! What are you going to do about it?" John was really into it. He was scary.

Allen held up his hands again. "I'm not sure what to say."

"What do you want to accomplish?" Susan asked.

"I want my immediate removal from this situation. Actually, I want John to calm down."

Susan was a great coach. "That's what you want to accomplish. What does John want to accomplish?"

"He wants to get his money back and flail some of my skin."

"John wants you to be aware of how upsetting and damaging this was. Does he feel that you empathized with how bad this was for him?"

"Probably not. Okay, here I go. That's sounds terrible, sir."

"You bet it was. Do I get my money back or do I have to go over your head? And I want some sort of compensation for my lost day of work."

"Sir let me apologize. This is not the kind of experience we want any of our customers to have. And certainly…"

Rudy formed a T with his hands, "Time out for a minute. Allen, you said, 'That sounds terrible sir,' and, 'Let me apologize.' Let's ask John if that fit the bill for empathy and an apology. John?"

"Yes. It sounded sincere."

"How about his apology?" Rudy asked.

"That was good, too."

Rudy continued. "Really? Allen only said, 'Let me apologize.' He didn't actually say, 'I'm sorry' or 'I apologize.' Allen, try apologizing again and then continue on."

"Okay. Sir, I'm sorry you missed your appointment and you wasted a day. I will certainly remove any charges. In addition, I'd like to make it up to you for your trouble. I want to keep you as a customer. If you don't mind, please tell me what you had to do to get help and I will make sure all your expenses are covered. Will that be all right?"

Bob held up his hands. "Stop there. Okay team, thoughts, reactions?"

Rose was first. "I thought it worked well, although John calmed down pretty fast. I think in a real-life situation he would have had a lot of time to build up a head of steam. The hear them out part of 'Take the H.E.A.T.' comes first because it usually takes a lot of hearing and little or no talking to help customers discharge their pent-up emotions. You can't resolve the issue during this listening step, but you sure can lose the customer by not listening well."

"That's the problem I had," Allen said. "I just wanted John to calm down and get the problem solved. Just listening seemed too passive. But I didn't know what to say to get things started."

"That's the point, isn't it," Rose nodded and smiled. "The customer with the beef should drive the conversation, not the employee who just wants to solve it and have the person go away."

Richard spoke up. "The customer isn't always right. John might have gotten angry enough to lose control. What do you do then?"

"I know," Susan said. "It's like with kids. You have to set limits. You tell the person that you can work with them, that you're on their side, but they have to calm down."

"Do you say, 'have to' to them?" Bob wondered. "Saying

'have to' to an angry customer is likely to fuel the flames and get, 'I don't 'have to' do anything!'"

"So, what do you say? Wait; let me answer my own question. You need to treat the person as an adult. Say something like, 'I'm on your side; can we work on this together?'" This last part of the role play opened up a lot of discussion. We all had a comment.

"I'd say, 'If you respect me, I'll respect you and we can figure this out.'"

"That sounds inflammatory."

"At what point do you just call the cops?"

"I think the worst thing you can do is send them to someone else to fix things and find that the other person isn't there. If that happens you've lost a customer forever."

"And it isn't linear. Sometimes you have to apologize three or four times during the discussion."

"And if they're not satisfied, they're going to tell ten others."

"How does Harnessing the Speed of Thought and the Four-Part Teaming Model apply to this?" Bob's question stopped our wandering. In less than five seconds, Harriet had an answer.

"On the face of it, the frustrated customer has a different issue and goal than an employee who just wants the angry customer to go away. The customer who is not treated well doesn't feel at all like a respected team member, feels no real influence, expects no real payoff, and believes he has to demonstrate a lot of anger to get someone to pay attention."

Bob continued. "Exactly right. Well done, Harriett. Take the H.E.A.T. is a good model to help you and the irate customer agree on the issue, create mutual goals and create a functional mini team. Same is true of the Four Cs. The extra factor highlighted in our loyalty bundle is the emotionality of human interactions, especially when the participants begin with vastly different issues and goals. Customers arrive with expectations and at least some investment just getting to your place of business. You already owe them when they step through the door. If you now frustrate them, you multiply your obligation to them. It's imperative to understand the impact of expectations on human dynamics and how employees must work with customers to meet their different needs."

"That's a heavy rap, man." I don't know how Rose came up with that particular comment at that moment, but that's what she said.

I thought it was heavy too and needed more explanation. "Who can expand on that?"

"I can," Rudy proceeded to explain, "The loyalty bundle creates loyalty. In simplest terms, loyalty is the willingness to return. A better and more stringent definition of customer loyalty is the customer's urge to tell others about your service or product and encourage them to buy. What we're talking about now, though, is what happens when you inadvertently mess up. Since none of us is perfect, customer loyalty includes a smidgen of forgiveness. And a degree of hope prompted by positive outcomes last time and promises about the next time."

"This is getting heavy again," Rose said.

"I will keep it as light as I can," Rudy promised. "In his book, *Discovering the Soul of Service*, Leonard Berry says that service is actually a promise. Loyalty arises from an accepted promise. Here it gets a little dicey but hold on. Loyalty is actually created only after a successful second promise."

"Heavy, heavy," Rose warned.

"It will make sense. You have customers because they believe your promise that they can get what they want from you. If they don't get it the first time, there is no loyalty and they go elsewhere. However, if they get what they want the first time, even if a mistake is made, they are more willing to believe your promise of next time and give you a second chance. If you fulfill that second promise, you begin to create loyalty. Mistakes, limited ones, are acceptable if you do the Four Cs and Take the Heat. However, loyalty is a bit hierarchical: loyalty based on price is weak; raise the price and loyalty might disappear. Loyalty based on quality or uniqueness is stronger. Loyalty based on your people is strongest of all. The first two Cs, connect human-to-human and collaborate, when done well, create loyalty to your people as they form a mini-team composed of your customer and your people."

"And the same holds true for creating employee loyalty to you, the boss." Bob added. Evidently, the guys were into lecture mode.

"Employees who are treated like robots will act like robots. Employees whose needs are met in every quadrant of the Four-Part Teaming Model become model employees." There was a universal groan at his pun, but he continued without pause. "Apply the Four Cs with employees, follow the Four-Part model and use taking the H.E.A.T. when necessary and you will create significant loyalty in your workforce. Remember, loyalty is trusting a promise you made. Know what that promise is and confirm that it is being fulfilled."

"Heavy," Rose concluded.

11

INTRODUCING A CHANGE

After a little catching up with each other at the beginning of our next collaborative, Richard flipped on an overhead that displayed this agenda and said. "I'm going to present how to introduce a change by having us all follow this agenda for change."

Agenda for Change

1. Welcome and set the stage
2. Introduce the change
3. Discuss the change
4. Agree on what we will do
5. Conduct a process check

He continued, "Thank you for being here. I'm always amazed at how much I enjoy the special qualities each of you brings to this collaborative. Particularly how you influence our learning by being so actively involved in any topic we discuss. Today our topic is introducing change, something we have all struggled with. I'm confident that at the end of the next 90 minutes each of us will be much more excited about and much more capable of introducing changes into our workplaces. Are we willing to proceed?"

All of us gave an enthusiastic thumbs up.

Richard continued, "Bob and Rudy asked me to propose a change they want to make in how we conduct our collaborative."

"Hold it right there, Mister!" Rose exclaimed. "You just used Rudy's Four-Part Teaming Model on us. Task, Membership, Influence, Reward... And it worked. I feel great. Very smooth, Richard, very smooth."

Richard smiled and nodded knowingly, "Here's the change. Each of us must bring a business colleague with us to the next two collaborative sessions. Not just anyone; it has to be someone who will likely want to participate in a collaborative themselves."

Using us to market the program? That didn't sound like our guys.

"In addition," Richard continued, "Rudy and Bob want each of these new colleagues to be senior executives in larger organizations so there is a greater likelihood that others within their companies might want to attend, too. Now, I can answer any clarifying questions you may have about the change Bob and Rudy want to implement."

I had to ask, "Why are they doing this? Sounds like blatant

commercialism to me."

Richard shook his head. "I can only answer questions for clarification, not the whys and wherefores."

Henry asked, "Does it have to be the same person at both collaborative sessions?"

"That's the kind of question I can answer. Yes, the same person. Any other questions?"

Nobody else said anything. The proposal was clear, or we were all stunned. We'd become a pretty close group with the two guys; now we felt taken advantage of.

Richard continued again, "Let's divide into two's or threes and talk only about what we like about this change. Then we'll report out to the large group. I've asked Bob and Rudy to listen in to help us stay on track. Remember, only what we like about the proposed change."

It wasn't easy at first because some of us naturally moved to what we didn't like. For example, the whole idea seemed wrong. And who has time to come to someone else's study group? But Bob and Rudy immediately reminded us to talk only about what we liked. So we did.

Five minutes later each group shared the things we liked about the proposal. Eliminating duplicates, this is what we listed:

> **What we like about this change**
>
> - Get more people to know the tools and concepts
> - Increase the guy's business
> - Maybe get a referral fee
> - Have others we can bounce ideas off
> - Improve business contacts
> - Share the wealth
> - Sell more of their books
> - Have us look wise and helpful
> - Get others' creative ideas

Then Richard said, "Now let's take five minutes back in our groups to discuss the challenges or hurdles we'll need to overcome to implement this change."

We did that and you know we expressed a few concerns but didn't get whiny about it.

Richard called us back again, and we listed the obstacles to implementation:

> **Challenges or hurdles**
>
> - Feeling like we're prostituting ourselves or maybe we're the pimps – hard to tell which
> - Extra work for us
> - May be hard to find someone willing to spare the time
> - Loss of trust that the guys are on our side
> - Just don't like the whole idea

"Based on our two lists, what should we do?"

This time we talked as a whole team. Comparing the positive and negative lists was interesting. The positives were more like outcomes and the negative list, the challenges, were more a listing of our feelings.

Despite our negative reaction, a few things on the positive list were interesting, like spreading the word and having more people become mistake-proofed leaders. I liked the idea of having more people available to bounce ideas off. The others were drawing the same conclusion.

Richard asked, "So, given our lists and our discussion, what are we willing to do to implement this proposal?"

After ten minutes more, we finally gave thumbs up to finding someone to invite as requested.

Richard then asked, "How about a process check? What did you like best about this way of introducing this change?"

Rose spoke up immediately, "I'm fascinated. At first, I was put off by the request. I thought how rude of Bob and Rudy to use us to market their program. As we went through the process, I saw that maybe it wasn't a totally bad idea."

Richard then asked, "And what would have made it even better?"

Jim said, "I'm not sure I understand all we did."

Richard put an overhead on showing the facilitator version of the agenda and clarified each point. "I remind you to look at this agenda as a bundle. Every part is essential, as is their order. Do all eight steps in this order."

> ### Agenda for Introducing a Change
>
> 1. Welcome participants and use the Four-Part Teaming Model to set the stage
> 2. Explain the change and answer ONLY clarifying questions. Do not discuss pros and cons
> 3. Break into groups of 2-3 and discuss ONLY what you like about the change. Then present to the whole group. List comments on flip chart.
> 4. Break into the same groups of 2-3 and discuss what you think will be challenging about the change. Then present to the whole group. Again, list comments on flip chart
> 5. Discuss what we should do to make the change based on the above
> 6. Agree on what we are willing to do to make the change
> 7. Conduct a process check about the change introduction: what they liked best; then what would have made it better.
> 8. Congratulate and thank the participants

"The first part of the meeting applies Rudy's famous Four-Part Teaming Model to get everyone prepared for the change. You then explain the change but don't answer any questions except to make sure everyone understands what the change is. This is critical.

If people want to express their opinions about the change, tell them they will have a chance to do so later during the meeting.

"We now apply 'Appreciative Inquiry' originated by David L. Cooperrider. It is designed to maximize productive discussion and minimize contention and debate, much like Harnessing the Speed of Thought. We break into small groups so everyone has a chance to express ideas and no one can just sit back and observe. Triads are often best. Everyone participates. First the positives. Always do positives first. This won't happen without facilitation like Rudy and Bob going around keeping us on track. Then have each triad report to the entire group and list their ideas on a flip chart so all can see. Something about hearing positives from each small group is magical. It's always impressive to hear how many positives people come up with even for the most difficult changes.

"Next, return to the small groups and list any challenges, hurdles, obstacles. Then present them to the larger group and list them on a flip chart.

"Hopefully, you have scheduled enough time during this meeting to determine what should be done to achieve the change and then have people declare what they are willing to do. Sometimes two or more meetings are necessary before all the steps can be completed.

"Finally, use a process check to acknowledge good work, clarify concerns, and then celebrate the team's success. I use this bundle in the army and was always amazed by how well it works."

Richard was obviously finished as we spontaneously applauded. "By the way," he said as we clapped and cheered, "You don't have to bring someone to our meetings. That was just a topic I thought would be controversial enough to get you a little hot." Those of us with empty paper cups tossed them at him.

* * *

On the drive home, I suddenly realized that except for a reminder or two, Bob and Rudy were almost silent. Richard facilitated the entire session using a model they had obviously coached him to use. As Rose would say, "Heavy."

12

ORGANIZATIONAL CHANGE

It was Richard again to report on this second session on change. "Bob Brown is my new hero," he began. "I don't think I have ever been as impressed with a book as much as his *The HST Model for Change*, especially his simple two-part approach. The guys had me read Kotter's *The Heart of Change* and other resources including ADKAR. I don't think any leader can lead change effectively without knowing all this material. If whatever you're leading isn't changing for the better, you're not really leading. My report has to do with how to use Bob's approach."

He had to have anticipated our reaction.

"Brownnoser."

"Teacher's pet."

"Booo."

He ignored the taunts, of course, and showed us this slide.

> **Bob's HST Model for Change**
> 1. The change has to make logical and emotional sense from beginning to end.
> 2. The change has to be done in teams led by a trained leader

"The first part," he said, "is simple. People who may be involved in any change are informed of a probable issue before any change is identified. No one is told, 'we're making changes around here.' That disenfranchises everyone and begins the well-known 'resistance to change' that doesn't have to happen. This means an organizational change begins with step one of the five steps of Harnessing the Speed of Thought, identifying the problem or opportunity. There is discussion and eventual agreement that an issue should be addressed. Both emotional and logical reactions are taken into account. The same goes for the four remaining steps of HST. Not doing anything different is always a possible solution. This approach creates a common list of facts.

"The second part includes Rudy's Four-Part Teaming Model. If everyone views the change as the compelling task and the effort is led by someone with vision, one who can inspire and lead teams, change will work. I want to explain the HST Model for Change with an example, a world-changing example."

Richard moved to his second PowerPoint image, a photograph of Dwight D. Eisenhower with his gleaming 4-Star rank insignia.

"As an army officer, I wanted to use as an example of large-scale change, the conquest of Europe beginning with the allied invasion of Normandy on June 6, 1944. It was a monumental effort, at great cost, for a precious and ultimately decisive grip on the continent.

"As we learned, Step 1 of HST is to identify the issue. Ike did this with his command team by emphasizing the current condition: (1) the Nazis were on the march and developing deadly rockets and even jet fighters; (2) the allied forces had been on alert too long and a delay would diminish troop readiness; and (3) taking action was dependent on a very narrow window in the weather. He ordered the invasion and his commanders responded."

"Everybody understood the need. That was simple: freedom and was both emotional and logical. Even so, you can understand that there was a wide range of feelings among the people. Someone made up the saying about American forces, 'They're overpaid, oversexed and over here.' I think Bob's emphasis on making emotional sense of change is especially important when identifying the issue and goal. People must believe in the need for change, and equally believe in the value of the outcome. It's part of what Kotter means when he says, 'see, feel, change.'

"The difficulty was to determine the strategies to implement.

Within the ranks of decision-makers, the leadership team had to sort the politics before much could happen. They had to agree to who would be in charge, what would happen after victory was achieved and who would control what land. Frankly, I can't imagine the conversations that were held, but it gives me an appreciation of how important it is to consider all the viewpoints and all the parameters. Exactly what Bob promotes."

The next slide titled Making Sense showed a World War II vintage sailor, cap at a jaunty angle, holding a finger to his lips and whispering, "Loose lips sink ships."

Richard continued, "World War II had at least two points of view, the side of truth and freedom and the side of truth and repression. Proponents of each side felt they were in the right. When we propose a change, we will also have two sides, those who want the change and those who don't, along with a bunch that just don't care.

"Basically, though, we must communicate the issue and define the goal in a way that shows people the benefits of making the change and helps them more easily give up something they valued before the change. We must anticipate questions and respond with good answers. And be clear about the goal and the work necessary to get there. Again, everything must make logical and emotional sense, to everyone, all the way."

Richard showed the next slide, a montage of hamburgers, hot dogs, bottles of soft drinks, a wine glass, large screen TV, computer, cell phone, golf club and a beach umbrella.

"Of course, at our level, we don't need quite the commitment of a soldier willing to die for his country. But we do need to keep employees invested and committed to the change. Our conversations must be clear and compelling and be able to compete with all the other messages they receive every day from co-workers, TV, the web and everywhere else. And we need to keep it up or people will fill the absence of information with whatever is available, true or not."

The next was a photo of what looked like a hefty-sized, middle-aged woman in a print dress holding a large pie in each hand, standing in front of a bombed-out house. Despite what looked like having lost her home, she was smiling. "This is my favorite photo. This woman's home was shelled by allied forces during the invasion. Despite the damage, she made pies she handed out to the Allied soldiers as they made their way inland past her home. When change makes emotional sense, even a woman who has just lost her home is jubilant. If it made only logical sense, this scene would not have happened."

He flipped to the next slide.

> Harrow School, 1941
>
> *Never give in, never give in, never, never, never, never - in nothing, great or small, large or petty - never give in except to convictions of honor and good sense.*
> Winston Churchill

"This is one of my favorite quotes. Winston Churchill said this to the students and staff of the Harrow school a year into the Battle of Britain. For me, this puts any change effort into perspective. How tough can change be when doing what we always did was leading to disaster? Tougher than we might think. The old way was a good way and people will have trouble letting go. We can never forget that change isn't always easy and is much harder if we're not sure we should be changing at all. It is much easier if change makes logical and emotional sense each step of the way *and* the leader helps us to remember that *and* we're in it together as a team."

The next slide was a photograph of an old basketball sneaker.

Richard pointed to the shoe. "This is to remind us that once we make a change, keep moving toward a meaningful goal. After the invasion of Normandy, it took another year to achieve final victory.

"The world is constantly changing, and we need to continue to ensure that the changes are the best for everyone. Despots are popping up all the time who enhance themselves at great cost to the lives and dignity of the rest of us.

"The same is true in business. Naysayers and the self-absorbed will constantly try to thwart the best intentions of the best leaders. We may have to revamp the issue and goal, revitalize our effort to understand hurdles and concerns, adjust our communication plan, and keep making sense of what we're doing.

"One concept to keep in mind is that people are always changing. What worked two months ago many no longer be right. Getting feedback along the way is critical. Leaders often are focused on working toward the outcome and forget about the process of change. Change is as much process as it is outcome. The process of making sense of change is necessary to enable change. And you make sense by communicating and receiving feedback. And I suppose I don't have to say it to this group, the communication and feedback must be sincere and meaningful, not checking boxes and regurgitating bullet points."

His last slide was a photograph of our group. "You remember when I took this picture? It was during our meeting when we were discussing if we were a team or not. I want to end my presentation by saying that we are a team, a team of leaders striving to become better leaders. I thought I was a well-trained leader before. Now I know that I am much better than I was. Thank you, Bob and Rudy, and thank you, team."

Richard bowed as we applauded. I was actually choked up. My dad's older brother was killed at Normandy. I never knew him, of course, yet talking about the invasion reminded me of the great cost of some changes. And, I suppose, the great cost when changes fail. Mistake-proofing leadership took on even more importance.

Rudy then stood and asked, "How do our two change bundles link together?"

Allen spoke first. "I think it's pretty simple. If the change is from outside, like a government agency telling you what you must do, then using the agenda for change is the way to go. If you are contemplating a change and have control over what and when, then HST is the bundle to use and then as you introduce the multitude of smaller changes, use the agenda for change again and again."

"But I think we can add more bundles," Sid said. "To do Bob's HST as Richard suggested, you can benefit from organizing a change team using Rudy's teaming model."

"I like this, and we can use a bit of John Kotter too," Harriet said. "Get your team together using Rudy's model, get them to mutually define the issue to be addressed and as they do, determine why this is the most urgent one to address right now.

"Have the team move to the goal which will also increase urgency by emphasizing the difference between the current problem and the wonderful future state. You can form a Kotter guiding team and create a vision. All the bundles can work together."

"Thanks, Harriett. That is exactly the way we want everyone to think," Bob said. "Although these tools and models can stand alone, sometimes we combine them. As long as we're managing a business that depends on people, we must be nimble, able to use whatever tool or combination of tools is best under the circumstances. In a way, we end up bundling our bundles. Agreed?"

It was thumbs up all around. Bundling our bundles. Mistake-proofing our leadership. It was coming together.

13

TIME

I do not want to wax too philosophical here, but when I saw "time" on our collaborative agenda, I decided to practice pondering again. When pondering was first assigned, one of my barriers was time; I didn't want to waste it. Sitting and just thinking didn't seem productive. I want my time to produce something.

As you know, I play golf. A time dilemma is the decision of going to the practice range or traveling out to the golf course. At the range, I hit eighty balls in about an hour. Eighteen holes and eighty strokes on the golf course takes about five hours.

In the same amount of time it takes to play eighteen holes I can hit eighty balls at the range and also read the paper, mow the lawn, have lunch, check the fluids in the car, drop off books at the library and help my kids with their homework. Obviously, the range is a more productive use of my time.

But hitting balls on the practice range does not seem as valuable to me as actually playing golf on a golf course.

In the big picture, my estimated time on earth is threescore and ten or maybe twenty years. That's the initial value equation. I'm assuming my productive years will add up to about forty. I'm comfortable with my personal vision statement. I have pretty clear career goals and I'm on target, so that's okay, at least for now.

Figuring an eight-hour day, just to keep things simple, I wonder how much of that time I'm adding value to my company and meeting the needs of my employees and customers.

How much do my employees think I'm worth? I have no idea, but I probably should. Do my customers get full value from my day's work? Probably not. Why not? Time. I don't use it as well as I could.

Do I work hard enough? You bet. I could work harder, but everyone knows the not so secret secret; don't work harder, work smarter. I'm haunted by Thoreau's one-liner, "The price of anything is the amount of life you pay for it."

We discussed time during the collaborative and how all of us wanted more. It was interesting that our group saw the same problem, never enough time, and the same solution, use our time more wisely, but none of us knew how to do that.

Rudy began his presentation on time by silently putting a grid on the flip chart, turning and then saying, "The answer to all your time constraints is within this grid.

This is Stephen R. Covey's self-management grid from *The 7 Habits of Highly Effective People*. Some of the examples are ours. Look at it for a while and you'll understand what to do."

He sat down and we all stared silently at the grid for a long time.

	Urgent	Not Urgent
Important	Quadrant 1 Crises Firefighting Deadlines Pressing Problems	Quadrant 2 Prevention Relationships Planning Learning Pondering Recreation
Not Important	Quadrant 3 Interruptions Some mail Some meetings Some reports Some calls	Quadrant 4 Trivia Busy work Some mail Some phone calls Time wasters

The pondering in quadrant two caught my eye.

Harriett broke the silence. "I see! I see! We spend our time in quadrant one, putting out fires when the quality work is in quadrant two."

"How can you not focus on the fires?" Sid asked. "You have to put them out."

No one answered his question. The guys remained silent. So we did too.

A couple of minutes went by. We were all staring at the grid as if the answer would somehow appear. Bob and Rudy just sat there.

Susan came up with a suggestion. "Let's take this logically. We want to avoid anything in quadrant four. It's not important and not urgent. It's waste. That's pretty clear. So, let's assume that in a perfect world, we totally avoid quadrant four.

Quadrant three is pretty much the same thing; it doesn't add much value. Don't do anything here unless you have run out of everything else to do. That leaves us with the important stuff; the value-adding stuff.

The trick, as I see it, is the difference between putting out a fire and doing quality work. If we do quality work, we'll have fewer fires to put out." She looked at the rest of us. "What do you think?"

I was thinking how I use my time. Seems like I spend much of it helping others who run into problems. Putting out fires. How could I avoid that? Better delegation? Better teamwork? Better problem-solving skills? Then it hit me.

"You know," I said, "the guys are exactly right," I motioned to Rudy and Bob, who were still quiet. "We can't control time, but we can absolutely control how we use it. We can choose to answer the phone when it rings or ignore it and spend the time, for example, figuring out the best way to delegate a task. We have to do only what is important and spend as much time in quadrant two as possible so we can then reduce the amount of time and effort that goes into quadrant one activities."

Bob finally spoke. "How do you do that?"

I was on a roll, so I stood up and went to the flip chart. "Let's list some ideas." The team started peppering me. Within three minutes I had a list of twenty-seven ideas. A few minutes later we had reduced it to ten.

Enhance Our Use of Time

1. Make sure you have clear value-adding goals and activities that help you achieve them.
2. Plan and set aside quadrant two time
3. Communicate the right stuff in the right way, no more or less than necessary
4. Write schedules in pencil; don't be married to everything
5. If it's not important now or in the foreseeable future, don't do it no matter how important it was yesterday
6. Schedule relaxation time and take it
7. Don't waste moments just because they are only moments
8. Keep track of your activities and move as much as possible to quadrant two
9. Teach others the Covey model
10. Do the same for all parts of your life

I sat down, quite proud of myself. "What do you think, guys?"

Rudy nodded to me but ignored my question. Instead, he asked, "Do you all get it?"

We chorused a strong, "Yes!"

"What quadrant are we in now?"

"Quadrant two!"

"Where do we belong?"

"Quadrant two!"

"Where do we want to be?"

"Quadrant two!"

"Where are we going to be?"

We all mumbled, "Quadrant one."

Rudy smiled. "You're probably right. But your job is to constantly work toward maximizing your quadrant two and that of your employees. And, because quadrant one also is important, your job when you must be in quadrant one is to do all you can to be effective in quadrant one. Next week we'll give you some more tools so you can do that."

For the umpteenth time, I couldn't wait for our next session.

14

COMMUNICATING

Unfortunately, I ended up missing the next meeting, which was frustrating because we only had three sessions left. I had to go out of town and caught a miserable cold that put me in bed for the next meeting. The guys did their best to catch me up, and I'm excited about what I learned about the communication bundle Allen presented.

From what I was told, Allen's presentation was a hoot. He dressed up in a tweed coat and came in pretending to smoke a pipe. Silently, slowly, he walked about studiously observing various details of the room and then paused and pointed his pipe toward the group. "You know," he said, "as a writer, I go to many parties. I was at one recently when a heart surgeon came up to me and said, 'You're that writer fellow, aren't you?' and of course, I replied in the affirmative. I no sooner got the words out when he said, 'I'm thinking that when I retire, I'll write a book or two, myself." To which I replied, 'That's funny. I was thinking that when I retire, I will do a heart surgery or two.'"

The point Allen wanted to make is that all of us communicate many times a day in many ways and consider ourselves pretty good at it; like a surgeon who thinks he can write a book just because he can write a sentence. We don't seem to appreciate just how hard it is to effectively communicate.

Allen listed the basic components of communication on a flip chart and said, "I know this seems elementary, but it poses a huge challenge.

> Basic Communication Elements
> - Sender
> - Intent
> - Content
> - Medium
> - Receiver

Then he turned and seemingly talking to himself continued, "People are incredibly complicated, and you may never understand them well enough to be a great communicator, which is why some businesses make a ton of money figuring out how to best advertise a product. And unless you're a professional, you may not have enough knowledge to always choose the best method of communicating. You also probably have limited choices like holding a meeting, writing a report or talking one to one. To top it off, very few people write or speak well enough to find the right words to express an idea in the best way." Allen shrugged his shoulders. "What to do? What to do?"

"First off," he suggested turning again toward the group, "assuming you as the sender want to communicate well, you must have clear intent. Is it information? Inspiration? Action? Second, carefully select the content of your communication based on what you want to achieve, your intent. And third, select the very best media you can based on your intent and your receiver's needs and characteristics, not what works best for you. Could this make up the communications bundle?"

Allen turned away from the group again muttering, "What to do? What to do?" Turning back, he stated emphatically, "This is not a mistake-proofed bundle! There is a fourth component, without which the bundle will almost always fail." He then went back to the flip chart and wrote:

FEEDBACK

"Without feedback, your message is like communicating into outer space. You have no idea if what you sent has even been received, let alone understood and acted on. How many memos and newsletters go out to no known effect? You must figure out the best way to give and get feedback from receivers so you can be sure your message has been received and have a chance to clarify it if needed. We cannot mistake-proof communication without an iterative feedback loop that ensures all involved end up on the same page. Also, using a standard template or sequence is useful. Medical people use something called SBAR, which stands for Situation, Background, Assessment, and Response when seeking clinical orders or transferring responsibility for a patient's care. For example, the patient can't breathe, this hasn't occurred before, I think it's an Asthma attack and I need your help to make sure I'm right.

"Mountain climbers make sure to call out things like "Climbing" and "Off-belay" so others can be sure of what's going on. Pilots use specific patterns of language to communicate with each other and with air traffic control." Allen gave a nod to Bob by saying, "Using the five Harnessing the Speed of Thought steps is a great way of effectively communicating with others." Allen then listed the communication bundle on a flip chart and sat down.

Communication Bundle

1. Have clear intent
2. Let intent determine content
3. Let receiver needs determine medium – use templates when possible
4. Have ways to receive and respond to feedback

Bob rose and said, "That's exactly right, four critical steps. I often use a simple method called the Ob-Quest technique for step 4. Ob-Quest is short for observation--question. The generic form of the technique is, 'This is how I see it. How do you see it?' and then go back and forth until all parties agree. This is a simple and direct way to give and get feedback."

* * *

Although all of this made good sense, I still wish I could have been there. The humor and emotion in Allen's presentation would have embedded the lesson more than just hearing about it. Even though I might not be totally recovered from my cold before the next collaborative, I was determined to be there for Susan's presentation on learning organizations. I knew very little about them.

15

LEARNING ORGANIZATIONS

When we initially received our assignments, Rudy said that Susan's was an almost impossible assignment. It was like asking her to design and build an ocean liner in the three weeks she had to prepare. Having read and pondered Peter Senge's *The Fifth Discipline,* the seminal book on learning organizations, Susan began her presentation.

"I would like to make three points. The first is that creating a true learning organization is incredibly important and incredibly difficult. Second, because many organizations have succeeded in becoming learning organizations, I believe that understanding the concepts and working to apply them is worth the effort. And third, well, I'll reveal the third point later."

"It's complicated material," she confessed. "The first major task is to understand the five disciplines that Senge says are a lifelong study and practice of a body of techniques. We all could spend a lifetime trying to master them."

She listed them on a flip chart and briefly described each by reading from her note cards.

> **Learning Organization Five Disciplines**
>
> - Personal Mastery
> - Shared Vision
> - Team Learning
> - Mental Models
> - Systems Thinking

"When we seek personal mastery, we engage in a quest for a personal vision, a clear view of reality and the choice to commit.

"Identifying and making explicit a shared vision focuses on heartfelt purpose, deep aspirations, shared meaning and alignment.

"We enhance team learning by suspending judgment, pulling together, and applying dialogue and skilled discussion.

"We apply mental models that enhance learning by discovering our untested assumptions, engaging in reflection and inquiry, discussing the impossible to discuss, and turning imagination into action.

"And lastly, we apply 'systems thinking,' the fifth discipline, by using complex system archetypes, reinforcing loops, balancing loops, and delays between cause and effect. It's complicated.

"And the complexity doesn't stop with the five disciplines. Senge also describes a learning organization architecture consisting of very specific guiding ideas, an innovative infrastructure, and theories and tools and methods: And a deep learning cycle comprised of new skills and capabilities that lead to enhanced awareness and sensibilities that lead to a change of attitudes and beliefs that lead to the acquisition of new skills and capabilities and so on."

Sid spoke up, "Isn't creating a learning organization like making any huge culture change that requires leaders to get the ball rolling and then use leadership bundles to help everyone else keep it rolling? Every concept and bundle that we've studied in this collaborative supports the creation of a learning organization."

Allen raised a hand and said, "I agree and also think that this collaborative is part of creating a learning organization. Our quest to become true leaders by using leadership bundles to mistake-proof our leadership behaviors clearly supports personal mastery. And, as we involve our staff in mistake-proofing, we enhance their personal mastery. It seems that the more working-together elements we define, the more we expect everyone to have a positive influence on the team, especially as situations and people change and hopefully improve."

Susan continued, "Yes, and our visioning process enables all involved to create a shared vision and work toward a common goal. Add the visioning to the Four-Part Team Model and The Five

Dysfunctions and you're in business with respect to both creating a shared vision and enhancing team learning.

"And with respect to mental models, our work with bundles has prepared us to embrace the learning organization mental models. For example, Lencioni's Five Dysfunctions support reflection, inquiry and resolving conflicts often based on what Senge refers to as 'undiscussables.' Also, Harnessing the Speed of Thought, the Four-Part Teaming model, and Covey's delegation model are all explicit mental models that reveal how we think and interact. When we use them in a mistake-proofing mode everyone involved knows the model and how it should be used.

"I had a bit of trouble with Senge's fifth discipline, 'systems thinking.' The best I can do is recognize that there are clearly identified archetypal patterns or system behaviors in organizations that explain many of the most persistent organizational mysteries and challenges. Many tend to foster behaviors that sustain current practices rather than promote change that improves them. If you recall in one of our meetings, we reviewed Barry Oshry's conceptualization of positions in organizations as tops, middles, bottoms and customers. His research shows that when people are dropped into any of these positions in a hierarchy, they will act the role predetermined by that position, not by their usual tendencies.

"It seems to me that the fifth discipline, systems thinking, enables us to explain behaviors that otherwise make no sense. With systems thinking we have some chance of responding in ways that can make a positive difference."

Susan concluded her presentation with, "Mistake-proofing leadership with respect to learning organizations requires leaders to master the learning organization disciplines and apply the leadership bundles we have been learning. This is a formidable quest, but it has great potential."

Susan gave a great presentation. As she ended, everyone stood and applauded. Perhaps as much for the power of what we had learned as the power of her presentation.

Rudy then asked, "Times about up, but before we go, who can tell us what we learned about mistake-proofing leadership as it applies to a learning organization?"

Rose ventured the concluding comment "Mistake-proofing is about applying leadership bundles bolstered by self-checks and successive checks. Although we talked about the five learning organization disciplines, the learning organization architecture, and the deep learning cycle, we certainly did not identify a learning organization bundle that we can easily apply. We did, however, see how we can apply virtually all the bundles we've studied to the task of creating a learning organization. I'm intrigued and intend to spend more time with Senge, especially systems thinking."

"Exactly," Rudy responded. "See you all next time."

* * *

At home, while continuing to nurse my cold, I had time to do more pondering. Prior to the collaborative, I hadn't fully appreciated how much I was leading primarily from brute force and position-power. And I either made things up on the spot or relied on what had worked before. Now I have models and know how to use them. My employees also are learning and using the models. Why had something so useful been such a long time coming?

I also thought about how our collaborative sessions were ending. I was going to miss my new friends, even though we talked a good story about keeping in touch. So much of the value of the collaborative was learning from each other's experiences. I learned about the need and value of compromise from Harriett who I think should run for President one day. Sid seemed to know everything there is to know about teamwork and every sport played throughout history. I felt small and selfish sometimes when John, the Scout leader, shared some of his experiences, but they did prompt me to volunteer for the first time in years. Susan taught me some great parenting skills; also, how much can get done in a day if you schedule right. I've never been much interested in the military, but Richard opened my eyes to the honor and intelligence required to keep us safe in today's world. And Allen, the farmer, who drove every week from Spokane, epitomized for me the character that won the West and has made America great. I hadn't known a farmer until we met, and I am very impressed. We should never lose people like him.

Rose has been my favorite. What a lady. She may be old, she may be small, but she was a giant in our collaborative. I don't think I've met anyone I've admired more. I think much of it is her presence. She is right there when you talk to her. Rose isn't playing a role or trying to be old and wise. She just is, like a mountain is just a mountain the second time.

With our reports completed, we planned to devote part of our final collaborative to celebrating and informally reviewing all we had covered. I looked forward to this but sensed that even with all I learned and the wonderful new friends I made; something was missing. I wasn't sure what it was, but I intended to raise the issue at our last meeting.

The guys also said they had one last thing for us to do. I imagined it was to review what worked and didn't work so they could better mistake-proof their collaborative on mistake-proofing leadership. Naturally, I was wrong. Surprised again.

16

MISTAKE-PROOFING MISTAKE-PROOFING

Our last meeting was held back at Rose's place. This time she went all out. There was the usual great coffee, tea and juices along with some of the best looking Danish, donuts, bagels and muffins I've ever had the pleasure of drooling over. There was enough food for twenty spread over a large table covered with a burgundy tablecloth and garnished with cloth napkins, real cups, glasses, plates, and utensils. There was even a flower bouquet of reds, yellows, pinks and blues in the center. "I know it is against the rules," Rose said, "So flunk me."

Rudy started the proceedings.

"I have a story," he said as he stood up. "I call it, *Propelled by Trust*."

"Many years ago, I bought a 30-acre farm near Lodi, California where my wife and I would grow our family. In the grassy yard on the east side of our tiny yellow farmhouse grew three tall black-walnut trees. Perfect for climbing. At the time of this story, we now had four children and our third, Troy, was 5 years old.

"One warm, sunny, summer day we were all in our yard, some playing catch, some on our tire swing, and Troy climbing the tallest tree. I stood below in case he slipped, which I doubted because he had proven his prowess as a climber on previous occasions.

"Suddenly, Troy began to jerk about, swatting at himself with one hand while clinging to a limb with the other, and all the while yelping 'Ow, ow, ow!' I couldn't see what the problem was, but I could see that he was greatly distressed.

"I immediately held my hands up toward him and yelled, "Troy, jump, jump! I'll catch you." Peering down from what I'm sure was a terrifying height for him, he jerked, swatted and yelped a few more times and then let go of the limb and leaped out of the tree.

"It seemed like he fell forever before I caught him. I quickly stood him on his feet, stripped off his striped T-shirt and discovered the problem—ants—a horde of giant, red, biting ants. I immediately brushed them off and shook out his shirt.

"As soon as I told Troy that all the ants were off him and his shirt, he pulled his T-shirt back on and headed out searching for another adventure, as though nothing had happened!

"Through the years, this memory of Troy's absolute trust in

me, his dad, has continued to warm my heart. He trusted me and I fulfilled my part. I don't know that anyone has ever trusted me as much before or since.

"The point is: (1) expect others to trust that you will do what you say you will do, and (2) never violate their trust.

"How about you? Have you ever trusted that much or been that trustworthy? It's all about allowing trust to propel action, yours and theirs." Rudy sat down.

We all silently turned in unison toward Bob.

He smiled. "Okay. I have a story too, about internal trust. My wife and I lived in Scotland in the early 1990s. I was trying to become a writer and was lucky to have a temporary appointment at the University of St. Andrews that gave us a little income and allowed the excuse to move over there and live in a 350-year-old stone cottage on the North Sea. The idea was I'd give it my all to become a writer, and we'd see what happened. Essentially, I quit my day job to take a flyer at writing the great American novel.

"For three hours in the morning and three in the afternoon, I'd sit at the computer piling up sentence after sentence. At this beginning stage, everything I wrote was golden. Not because it was good, but because it was adding toward the seemingly impossible eighty thousand words I needed to complete a novel.

"Each morning I would read yesterday's output, shrug my shoulders, sigh, then press on. After about three months and upwards of fifty thousand words, I had the courage and finally the clarity of thinking to delete the bad stuff. I lost over half of what I had written. Perhaps a better word is discarded. What I 'lost' was junk, but it took a while for me to learn that. In hindsight, I held onto every word for fear I wouldn't be able to write enough of them to make a novel. I had to learn to trust that I could, or if I couldn't, so be it. Within weeks of acquiring this bit of writing wisdom two marvelous things happened.

"The first had to do with one of my characters. At that time, he was a minor character, a support for the protagonist's work as a research scientist. The minor character was a lab assistant who also was an animal rights activist. My plan was for this minor character to change some data to ruin one of the experiments. But one afternoon, as I was typing, this character planned his sabotage and then quickly burned down the entire laboratory. This was not my idea. My character had taken over the story.

"The second event also had to do with a character, but one much more under my control. I had one of my characters kill someone. This may not sound like a big deal, especially in a murder mystery. For me, however, I was concerned about my responsibility to my characters and my readers. I couldn't just kill off a character without good reason, and I couldn't give my readers a large body count just for the fun of it. It is simple to write a sentence to drown someone, to stab them to death, or even have them be slowly and agonizingly strangled. But my characters are important, and more than that, I have an obligation to my readers to give them something that wasn't gratuitous.

"I pondered that obligation for a long time. I was responsible to my readers when I was writing, when they read, and whenever anyone might pick up one of my books years and years later. I had to work hard to choose the right word and put together the best sentence for this fantasy world. And, the importance of my effort doesn't end. A reader starts a book being promised that the investment in the story will turn out to be beneficial hours and hours later. I had to allow a degree of letting go to write well, yet at the same time put in as much effort as I could. That was the real lesson for me, and I think there is a lesson there for you, too. In real life, you must give it your all and enable others to do the same. You have to put in before you take out. Your followers, like my readers, deserve your best.

"Clarity of purpose, trust, including others, truly caring are all important and I hope we have helped you see that a bit better. You cannot do it alone and you have to use the right tools. Do you have the right tools?"

Thus, began our review of the material. Everyone had a lot to say about, "Yes, we have the right tools." Then it hit me.

"Guys," I said, "You have done a great job explaining how to mistake-proof our leadership using all these tools. But for the last week or so, I felt there was something missing and I just now figured it out. You have given us tools, but you haven't taught us how to make our own tools. Is that a reasonable request? How did you decide which bundle to use for mistake-proofing, and can you share that with us?" The others murmured their agreement.

Bob said, "Uh, oh." Rudy looked worried. "Bob?" he said. "Rudy?" he replied. Rudy then went over to a flip chart and pulled the first blank sheet up and out of the way. Already written on the next sheet was this:

> How to create a Mistake-Proofing Bundle

That was pretty cool. They set us up. But I don't know-how.

"Let's do some team thinking," Rudy suggested. "Divide into two groups and see if you can come up with the five elements that will help you create a Mistake-Proofing bundle."

I got together with my good old Rose, Sid, and Harriett.

"We'll give you ten minutes," Bob said. "That should be plenty for great minds like yours."

I love these exercises. They allow us to formulate ideas together and we always want to beat the other team. This time both groups put our thoughts up at the same time.

> Measurable
> Feedback
> Integrated steps
> Subsequent checks
> Documented effectiveness
> Use in different settings
> Clear objectives

> Feedback
> History of use
> Well known
> Can be tested on the job
> Checks
> Credible

My group contributed the top list. Neither group stuck to listing five as Bob suggested. I guess by this time we were all pretty rebellious.

Bob looked over the list, taking his time. He slowly turned toward us. "Okay, smart alecks. Exchange lists and see if you can follow directions this time. Edit the lists down to the top three, not including feedback that's already on both lists. Feel free to alter them if needed to explain them better. Put feedback at the top of both lists."

So we went back to our teams and came up with the following.

> Feedback
> Well known
> Credible
> Can be tested on the job

> Feedback
> Clear objectives
> Use anywhere
> Integrated steps

"Okay, team," Bob said. "If you want to accept the challenge, everyone work together to reduce these two lists to what you believe would be the three necessary and sufficient elements to mistake-proof leadership for now and into the unknown future. We'll give you twenty minutes."

We were off like a pack of greyhounds. None of us said it, but I'm sure we wanted to come up with the three elements in less than twenty minutes.

I suppose it was only natural for my team to use our list as the basic list and evaluate the relative merits of the other list. Likewise, our honorable opponents looked with a critical eye at what we listed. With all due respect and camaraderie, we quickly debated which elements on each list were the best. This went on for five or six minutes.

Suddenly Rose stopped us. "Wait a second," she said. She looked over to Rudy and Bob who were sitting quietly at the far end of the table. "Look how the guys are just sitting there like they know something we don't. They haven't said a word."

"They do know something we don't," Harriett laughed. "That's why we're here."

"What are you thinking?" Sid asked Rose.

"I think we fell into some kind of trap."

The way Bob and Rudy sat there, I had to agree something was up. It came to me. We were debating. So that's what I said. "We're debating."

Rudy raised an eyebrow. Bob just sat there.

The group murmured agreement. Someone said, "We should be harnessing the speed of thought."

So we did.

"What's the issue?"

"How to mistake-proof leadership?"

"Is that it?"

"How about, 'How to create mistake-proofing tools?'"

"We were talking about mistake-proofing bundles."

"I think what we want to do is bigger than that."

"Bigger than just bundles?"

"Yes. I think what we have to figure out is how to mistake-proof our leadership beyond what we learned in the collaborative. So we can mistake-proof in ten years."

"That's right. Things change. Maybe bundles will change."

"Then we're back to the issue of mistake-proofing our leadership."

"I can go with that. All agreed?"

We all agreed. We next tackled our goal. Since we applied our combined brainpower to the effort, it took only a couple of minutes to declare the goal was to mistake-proof our mistake-proofing.

The guys still hadn't said a word, but I think I could see them smiling.

The group listed about ten hurdles, none of which seemed to

prohibit us reaching our goal. After another five or six minutes, we had brainstormed three solid ways to mistake-proof our mistake-proofing.

> **Mistake-proof our mistake-proofing**
> 1. Use well-defined, evidence-based bundles
> 2. Measure processes and results
> 3. Put "andons" in place and use them

"We're done," Sid announced.

The guys got up and stood looking at our list.

They studied it for a long time. They began nodding their heads. "Bravo," Bob said. They turned and started applauding. Rudy looked at Bob. "Our work here is finished."

"I agree," Bob said. They shook hands and walked out of the room.

We were silent, thinking they would be back immediately. But they didn't come back.

Richard laughed. "I think this might be a 'see-feel-change.' Let's grab some more of Rose's wonderful refreshments and take a break. I guarantee they will be back in five minutes. I hope."

They weren't.

After ten minutes they still had not returned. We began to

wonder. Richard poked his head out the door and saw nothing. There was a half-hour left of our meeting time. Just when it seemed they wouldn't come back, they did, Rudy carrying a cardboard box.

"Hi, team," Bob said.

Rudy put the box on the table. "We come bearing gifts," he said.

"If," Bob added, "you can complete your great work on mistake-proofing mistake-proofing."

"And how do we do that?" Richard asked.

Rudy immediately answered. "You can simply accept our recommendation and then explain how it all works. The recommendation is to add one more element, 'view,' meaning the leader has to understand the situation, the goals, personal strengths and weaknesses.

Basically, to mistake-proof leadership, you have to ensure the absolute best perception and perspective and then apply the tools you mentioned."

That sounded good to me. I've always been amazed by leaders who just seemed to know what they needed to know. I guess that's perception and perspective, and we may as well call it 'view.'

Bob added, "Get together and discuss the four parts of mistake-proofing mistake-proofing and present your ideas. Rudy and I will enjoy more of these great muffins while we finish the orange juice."

We quickly decided that I would present the new view idea,

Harriett would do bundles, Rose the measurement of processes and results, Richard the "andon" and everyone else would contribute whatever they had to say as we went along. It looked like this.

Mistake-proof Mistake-proofing

1. Have a clear view
2. Use well-defined, evidence-based bundles
3. Measure processes and results
4. Put "andons" in place and use them

"My point about view is that a leader must be able to conceptualize the situation now and how it will best play out. There must be an accurate assessment of strengths and weaknesses, what the competition is all about, available resources and all the other practical matters of business. The leader has to make sure there are no blind spots or fantasy-based assumptions. Without the right view, a leader could apply the steps of a bundle exactly right, but it could be for the wrong issue and the wrong time to use it."

Harriett explained our thoughts about bundles perfectly. "Bundles are the best evidence-based thinking at the current time applied through a collection of skills that help accomplish a defined task and reach a defined outcome. The leader needs to make sure that a particular bundle is the correct one to use and then ensure that each element of the bundle is applied and applied correctly."

"Without using every element of the bundle, you're reducing the probability of success," she continued, "and you must follow the standard so you can do a self-check and others can do successive checks. Our current issue with bundles is determining how we can successfully use a bundle that wasn't covered in this collaborative or perhaps one created a year or five years from now. It seems to us," she nodded at the rest of us, "that a bundle is simply the best evidence-based thinking of how to do something that has discrete elements that can be identified, communicated, performed and measured so the bundle will be used successfully."

Sid sagely offered, "A bundle is a collection of the necessary and sufficient actions to accomplish a task or reach a goal."

Rose then segued perfectly into measurement. "For most things in business, if you can't measure it, it is next to impossible to improve it. One of the benefits of using leadership bundles is the transparency that allows everyone to know if the bundle was used or not and whether the bundle accomplished the defined goal. The idea is to make the issue crystal clear, the goal defined in measurable terms, the bundle elements specific, and the results obvious so everyone can both measure and improve them."

Richard presented our thinking on "andons," a topic that was discussed during the meeting I missed. "The classic definition of an andon is that it is a signal, usually a lighted but sometimes an aural warning of a current malfunction in a process. It is designed to alert the team to emerging problems so the problems can be addressed immediately. The idea is that no matter how well designed a process, or a leadership bundle might be, yesterday's success is no guarantee of success today. We must be on constant alert. To mistake-proof leadership, we must design ways to continuously warn us of an impending mistake. This could be as simple as an employee satisfaction board indicating each employee's satisfaction at the end of each shift, or as complicated as a visibility dashboard displaying a dozen or more activities."

Richard sat down when he finished and we all silently looked at the guys. They looked at each other. Bob asked Rudy, "What do you think?" Rudy said, "Time to party."

Bob raised his index finger, "But, in an organized fashion. Rudy, would you do the honors?"

"I would be honored to do the honors." Rudy reached into the box he was carrying and pulled out a certificate. "We have a bundle for celebrating the end of a collaborative and it is comprised of three elements. First is recognition of your outstanding contribution to this collaborative. You each get a certificate. Second, and this is very important, we use the Four-Part Teaming Model. Third, we take time to enjoy each other's company. This is a bundle that can, maybe should, be used at the conclusion of any significant project.

"I will hand out the certificates to each of you and as I do, I'll mention just one reason why you are a great member of the team. After I do that, I want you to give us one personal reward that you gained from being on the team. I also want to point out that the compelling task has been to become true leaders and that your influence on the team has been your honest expression of ideas and feedback. This team has been outstanding."

Rudy walked over to Susan and handed her a certificate. "Susan, you're first so you have the least amount of time to think of a personal reward. While you do, I want to say that one reason you have been such a great team member is that you have helped us keep in mind the human values of kindness, service and integrity that make all this effort worthwhile. Thank you."

"Thank you, Rudy and Bob. This has been a wonderful experience. I really enjoyed it. As for a personal reward, I must say that everything I learned has been a personal payoff."

"More specific, please," Bob told her.

"More specific. Okay. I have confidence that when I go back to full-time work, I'm going to knock everyone's socks off."

We all cheered. Rudy went to Allen. "Allen, thank you very much for being with us. You brought a special kind of wisdom, a practical perspective that only a farmer can have; but also, by traveling so far each week you affirmed that what we all were doing together is important. Thank you."

"You're welcome," he said. Allen then looked over to Bob. "And to be specific as to my reward, I have a much better idea of what leadership is. I was hoping to learn how to work more effectively with my hires, but I have learned how to work better with everyone. That's a huge payoff."

"Richard," Rudy said, giving Richard his certificate. "Your being on the team enriched our understanding of leadership, humane leadership, crisis leadership, leadership that can win wars and keep people alive, or do the opposite. Without you, I think many of our conversations would have been more academic and less real-life. Thank you."

"Thank you. I gained a lot too. Most important to me is to see leaders from many walks of life. My life is very focused and structured. It was enlightening to learn how other people view the world and how to make it better. This has been extremely valuable to me."

Rudy moved to Harriett. "Keeping with our government theme, here is your certificate Harriett. I believe our team was improved by your experience and stories of political in-the-trenches struggle and compromise. A true leader has to have true followers and I think you have helped us understand how that process works."

"And I can say just one reward?"

"Yes," Bob answered. "Unless your other rewards are really good."

She smiled. "They are, but I'll keep it to one. My single greatest reward from being in this collaborative was learning about Harnessing the Speed of Thought. I have used it every day since you presented it to enable people with different views to work together effectively. That and the Four-Part Teaming Model. It works really well too, to bring people together."

It was my turn. Rudy handed me my certificate and said that I contributed the most logical business orientation they have ever encountered, as befitted a computer business guy. I told the team that I gained a new appreciation for learning. Not that I thought I knew it all, I said, but I hadn't realized that learning experiences could be so well structured and be so quickly rewarding. I could see Bob and Rudy liked hearing that.

"I guess I'm next," John said as Rudy handed him a certificate.

"John, as the father of two Eagle Scouts, I want to say that what you brought to our team was the gift of honor. With every discussion I could see, I think we could all see, the effort you wanted us to make to ensure our tools were used to do the right thing. You held our feet to the fire to tell the truth, to honor each other, to strive for the greater good."

John blushed. "Thank you. In return I met a wonderful group—no, a team—and learned so much, much more than I could have dreamed. What I got was, I guess I can say it, renewed faith that we adults are working to make this a better world for our children and grandchildren. What else is there?"

"Thanks, John. Sid, here is your certificate and congratulations. You, too, have a youth orientation and combined with John to help us see a bigger picture than just profit and market share. In addition, you reminded us of insights athletes seem to learn, 'perfect practice makes perfect.' I don't think any of us will forget the value of practicing and keeping our eye on the goal."

"Thank you. Okay, for my single reward, I would have to say it was learning more about the importance of the people part of it. I have always emphasized skill training. Now I realize that team functioning may be even more important. That's the key takeaway for me."

"Thank you, Sid. So, we come to last, but not least, Rose, today's host." Rudy handed her a certificate. "Rose, you have brought wisdom to our team. I don't think I can say it any better or clearer. We have been very lucky to have shared in your experiences and your insights. Thank you."

Rose smiled. "Thank you, too. Thank you all. For me, the best reward has been the joy of learning and doing with a wonderful team of people. I can think of no better use of my time than to be here with all of you."

Bob stood up. "That was amazing. Thank you all. Now let's celebrate."

We relaxed, we ate and drank, we chatted and had a good time. But if I had known then what I know now, I would have been heartsick, probably unable to do anything but sit and stare.

17

ROSE

Five weeks after the end of the collaborative, Rose and I were having lunch in the Blue Burrito, the same place we lunched during our first-day intensive session. We caught up each other while waiting for our food to arrive. As soon as it did, Rose told me the reason we were meeting. "I want you to be my coach," she said.

I was flattered. "I would be glad to be your coach, but I don't think I know more than you do about anything, so it might be a bit hard. Do you have something specific in mind?"

"Yes, I do. I want you to be my coach as I use a few of our leadership bundles to make sure I'm doing as well as can be done."

"I think I can do that."

"But I need to explain something to you." She took a deep breath. "This may be more difficult than I thought. As you know,

I'm old and old people are supposed to get sick and be on their way. According to my doctors, that's what I'm doing."

Oh, oh, I thought. I didn't like what I was hearing. "I'm not sure I understand what you mean."

"Of course, you do. I'm old, I'm sick and I'm dying. That's why I need a coach."

I didn't know what to say. I didn't know anything about dying.

She seemed to read my mind. "I don't need a coach for dying. I can do that on my own." She quickly added, "I need a coach to make sure that I'm doing what I need to do well, while I can still do what I need to do."

"Rose."

"I know this is a shock, and I'm sorry. But I thought you might get a kick out of helping me, and I'm choosing you because I think you're the best person for the job."

"I don't know what to say."

"Well, then, I'll keep talking. I want you to coach me on using two of our leadership bundles. I'll do a self-check certainly, and I will have others do successive checks. But I want you to do successive checks, too, and coach me to do everything right."

"Rose, I'm so…"

"What two bundles do you think I want to use? Any guesses?"

"Rose…"

"I know. I'm sorry. It's quite a shock. I have the advantage. I learned about my condition a week after the end of the collaborative. It took me a while to understand that I didn't have a lot of time to play the role of a wise old lady."

"How much…"

"Couple of months or so, not much more."

"Rose, I'm so sorry."

"Thanks. I'm okay." She said it softly, but she did sound okay.

"What can I do?"

"For starters, can you guess which bundles I want to use?"

"Rose, I don't know. This is all…"

She smiled. "I'm just trying to keep things light. What I want to do is help my family deal with what is going to happen, both personally and business-wise. I have been the controlling force in so many areas, and others are going to have to step up to the plate. So, this will be obvious, the two bundles I want to use are the change bundle and the delegation bundle."

I had to smile. "Makes sense Rose and I will be honored to be your coach. How do you want to do this?"

"I'll put together a plan, and I'd like to meet once a week to go over what I'm doing. We can do that by phone or in person, but I'd much prefer that we get together."

"Okay. Want to meet here at the BB?"

"That would be nice."

"Do you want help with the plan?"

"I'd like you to review it when I have it finished. Otherwise, this is something I want to do on my own, but I want your input before I act on it. I don't think they give do-overs with this kind of thing."

"Oh, Rose." This was breaking my heart.

"Now, now, don't fret. When you're old, this isn't as bad as you might think. I had the chance to do some wonderful things and still do. I have the time and the resources. Most people don't get that. I'm thankful. Keep your mind on the task and we'll both be fine. Are you okay with this?"

I was.

We agreed to meet same time, same place the next week.

* * *

I arrived first and had to wait about ten minutes. It was the longest ten minutes I can remember. Would she look drastically different? Would she be functioning okay? Would she have a reasonable plan? What if she didn't? Should I be in contact with her family? Should I consult with Rudy and Bob?

Before I had a chance to answer my own questions, in struts the Queen of the Blue Burrito. I should have known better. Rose wore that red dress, lighting up the room as she walked to the table. We chatted for a while until Rose declared what she wanted from today.

"I'd like to tell you about change today, then next time or maybe the time after that talk about delegating. Okay with you?"

I nodded. "Okay with me."

"I like the HST Model for change. It certainly applies here. However, the issue that my family is identifying is not the right one. I want them to focus on taking over my obligations. They're only worried about my dying. They have the picture wrong."

I had to smile. Of all the people I knew, only Rose could get frustrated at her family for worrying about her dying when there was a business to run. "So, you haven't been able to create a mutual definition of the issue yet?"

"Not the right one. They're running around trying to make me comfortable, planning to make my last days meaningful and pretty much ignoring the huge hole I'm going to leave."

"Maybe you've already helped them handle the business issues of you not being there. But, as your coach, I think you are exactly right, you must make sure all see the issue the same. You might want to identify a few separate issues, personal and business, that will have to be addressed."

"Yes, keep the business and personal separate. I can do that. I probably should have two issues and goals, for business and for personal issues. I'll set that up. Do you think HST will work here?"

"Absolutely. I think this is a grand use of Bob's model."

We continued talking about Bob but didn't get into any more detail of his model. I think that Rose just wanted to connect with someone outside the issues she was working on. As soon as I realized that, I thought about the Four Cs of the loyalty bundle. It was odd to think of them in this context, yet at the same time, they seemed like a very helpful set of things to do. I would connect. I would collaborate. I would contribute to the last ounce if that's what she needed. And I would make sure to confirm satisfaction.

The next week she had her two approaches and who would do them in place. For business, she chose her son, the current company vice-president, her older daughter, the power behind their real-estate empire, her middle grandson who was a senior in business school and Beth, who she confessed to me was her favorite grandchild and who was still in high school.

"Why Beth?" I wondered.

Rose smiled. "Beth is a dear. I want her to feel like she's making an important contribution and I think this will do it. That and I believe she will help keep her elders focused on the important things. They already have agreed on a goal, 'We will operate as if Rose was still here.' And we're already including everyone in the process. All the parts of the supply chain are aware of what is happening. That feels quite strange, let me say, but we agreed that letting everyone know was necessary. We're waiting to hear back so we can assess barriers. How am I doing coach?"

"Great. I'm impressed. What about the other personal team?"

"You sure don't let an old lady rest on her laurels, do you? The personal is going, though I don't think quite as well. Someone dying is a delicate thing for most people to discuss, especially with the one dying. I think we're okay though."

"Tell me more."

"Team: my younger brother, my younger daughter and two grandchildren. Solid, intelligent, motivated and only a little scared. I think I have the right people."

"The right people because they're intelligent, motivated and only a little scared?"

"That and they were the only volunteers."

"Any goal yet?"

Rose laughed. "I can't tell them, but I can tell you. The goal I have is me lying totally relaxed in my coffin without a care in the world, no worries about my family at all. That is a nice image, but not a vision they would like."

"Did you talk about a vision?"

"Oh, yes and we have one too. Now you must understand my family. We don't seem to be like a lot of other people."

"I can imagine."

"So the vision they created for my upcoming journey is, 'Granny is going to go with her boots on and her hair flying, leaving stories that will be told for twenty generations.'"

"I like that," I told her.

"I do too. It almost makes it worth it."

She seemed too okay for me, so I asked. "Rose, are you really okay?"

"Yes, I really am." She reached over and patted my arm. "I have lots of people to talk to and lots of work to get done. And I have you to coach me."

Over the next three weeks, we met at the same time and the same table. After our meetings, I would walk her to her car. I could see that she was becoming weaker, but she was no less a presence. She told me how she handled a delegation meeting with her older daughter Deanna.

Rose began without ceremony as usual. "Deanna, I want to delegate most of my current responsibilities to you. Are you okay with that?"

Deanna smiled. "I'm more than okay. I've wanted to do more, but you do it all so well and I didn't want to interfere. I appreciate that you want me to take over some of your duties. I'm ready."

"Are you familiar with Covey's delegation model?"

"Mom, you taught it to me."

"Indeed, I did. How shall we use it?"

"Well, as I was taught, it is a good idea for the delegator and the delegatee to mutually decide on each element."

"Do you have a preference for how we do it?"

Deanna suddenly looked serious and sad. "My preference is that I wish you didn't have to delegate."

Rose smiled at her daughter. "I know, sweetheart. But let's use the model and get done what needs to get done. That's part of the benefit of using a model; it can work no matter what else may be going on. How about I define the desired result and you define the rest and let's see if we can agree."

"That sounds good. So, define the result."

"The goal that I am delegating to you is to accomplish two things: you are comfortable handling our real estate interests and the rest of the family realize that these interests are in better hands next year than they were this year."

"Mom, that'll never happen. How can you say such a thing?"

"Those are the desired results. You have a problem with them? Let's talk."

"You can't be replaced."

"I'm not saying I can."

"What are you saying?"

"That you can step up and do more than you may have thought possible. Sweetheart, my getting old and sick and dying is one thing; you running the show is something completely different. Can you accept that you have much to offer that you haven't offered yet?"

Deanna nodded. "Yes, I think that's true. I'm glad you noticed."

Rose continued, " …and that someone, namely me, has been a small but dogged hurdle?"

"Not a hurdle. You ran the company."

Rose silently looked her daughter in the eye for a moment. "And can you honestly say that it is time, if not past time, for me to step aside? The truth, now."

"Yes. But that the time is right for me to take over, not for you to step aside."

Rose went on to describe how she and her daughter discussed the daughter's expanding role in the property business and Rose's comfort in letting go. "I see more and more," Rose said, "of the value of having a model to almost eliminate the distractions of the human element in tough discussions while at the same time supporting the human element by using all the parts of the bundle."

Rose and I continued meeting each week, but she soon arrived as a passenger in a car driven by one of her grandchildren. She continued to look regal as I helped her out of the front seat.

I asked her one day why she thought she needed coaching. I suspected that I had not provided nearly as much as I hoped I might and also worried that I had offered less coaching than she expected.

"My dear friend," she answered. "You have been all the coach I could ever imagine having and exactly what I asked for."

"All I seemed to do was listen."

"You have done far more than that. Every time I used one of our bundles you confirmed I was using it in the right situation and using it correctly. You confirmed what I was doing was the best that could be done. What I am doing right now is the most profound activity anyone could do. I know my time is severely limited. Every decision I make about anything is probably my last. I am saying goodbye to the people I love and conducting business at the same time. I'm either a saint or a Scrooge; I don't know which. You, my friend, have given me perspective, a rare and priceless commodity."

"Just by listening?" I said, with some disbelief. I thought she was just being kind.

"Don't sell coaching short." There was an edge to her voice. "We learned about mistake-proofing leadership and that means the necessity of successive checks. Do you think I want my last efforts with my family to be guesses?"

I felt totally humbled. She was right. If we take anything seriously, we also must figure out how to do it the best it can be done. I wasn't just a pleasant lunch companion to a nice old lady. I looked at Rose with a new awareness. "You wanted me to help you do what needed to be done exactly right. I finally get it. Right now is the most important time of your life. You trusted me to say what needed to be said."

She reached out and touched my hand. "I didn't want someone to agree with me. I wanted someone who could help me be better, to not make a mistake in the most critical areas of my life. You have done a superb job."

I felt great but suddenly was suspicious. "Wait a second. You said a long time ago, when we first met, that you wanted to pass on real wisdom." I tilted my head and narrowed my eyes. "Was I a student in all this, too? Was this your way of passing on wisdom?"

She laughed. "I hope you don't mind. I have been impressed

by your intelligence and your character. I knew you were successful, but maybe you needed a bit more clarity of purpose. I needed you as a coach and thought, at the same time, that perhaps there was something you could learn on our little journey together."

"Do I see a mountain or no mountain?"

She patted my hand. "You see a mountain again," she declared. She reached for her coat. "But I fear that I must go. There is so much I must do, and my time is more and more limited just as my energy seems to fail so much quicker. My friend, I'm afraid this has to be my last coaching session."

I half-heartedly protested. She had clearly declined in the past few weeks. I walked her to the car and gave her a hug before she got in.

She rolled down the window of the car. "Thank you, Andrew."

"You're welcome, Rose."

The car disappeared around the corner.

18

A CALL TO ACTION

A year has passed since the collaborative. Probably because of its intensity, I still keep in touch with everyone—everyone except Rose, whom I think of often. We talk about our progress becoming true leaders, and I know that each of them agrees with what I'm about to share with you.

The key for me in becoming a true leader is the reality of bundles, bundles of behaviors and bundles of people. Each is essential as I attempt to mistake-proof my performance as a leader.

I've enlisted the help of my employees and they frequently comment on how they, our customers and our processes benefit from how well I'm mistake-proofing my leadership. I know I'm good alone, but rarely good enough. The lingering image of a basketball shooter intent on making baskets reminds me to always get feedback. What success I achieve is a shared success.

For me, the most powerful tool the guys presented is Rudy's Four-Part Teaming model. I use it in one form or another almost every day. I'm convinced that all leaders should do the same. The impact on how people work together is astounding.

And after considerable practice, I now use Bob's Harnessing the Speed of Thought in most of my thinking, communicating, and group activities. It easily cuts through many human inefficiencies. If you use just these two models, you're halfway to the mountain Rose talked about.

Every day I see evidence of how much I learned in the collaborative in the models and tools I use. I don't know if I can overemphasize the value of using models and bundles of behaviors.

For much of my career, I relied exclusively on my own intelligence and a few ideas that dated back to college. If that worked, fine; I'd keep doing it and never consider the probability there were better ways.

In a way, I was acting from the perspective of "don't fix it if it ain't broken." That kind of thinking doesn't get anyone, anywhere. I now know that models and bundles give us well-defined actions that lead to improved results. Outcomes can always be improved, especially if you have an idea of what to do and how to measure results.

I've also deepened and anchored my understanding of the mistake-proofing material by teaching and coaching others. This alone has moved me closer to being a true leader. I encourage you to do the same.

I'll finish by acknowledging that before the collaborative I rarely applied any form of Lean Thinking to what I was doing. Since the collaborative, I've extended my exploration of this approach. The guys did a brief introduction, but Bob has much more to say about Lean in his books. Reading and applying this material has been a productive use of my time.

So how about you? You've read the book, tested the material and, I expect, found it useful. The key now is, don't stop learning and changing. Mistake-proofing your own leadership actions will unleash the leadership of others and enable you to truly make a difference.

Part II

REFLECTIONS

REFLECTIONS

It sounds harsh to say, but most leaders are nominal leaders, leaders in name only. They rely too much on what worked once and do not update their learning with what works best. In contrast, true leaders continually refine their leadership skills to achieve their goals and enable followers to benefit from the effort and the journey. They honor their obligation to ensure that they are leading toward the right goals in the right way. We intended that our readers learn enough from our presentation to successfully apply the presented concepts and models.

To be a true leader, you must know the models, know-how and when to use them, and ensure that followers are part of your mistake-proofing process. Here are some of our further reflections.

THE INVITATION

Our narrator's initial response to the collaborative invitation is typical of nominal leaders. He recalled from some distant memory that most learning events had not benefited him. Simultaneously, he forsook any personal responsibility for his lack of learning, rejected the possibility of another event providing value, and determined to continue doing what he was already doing. All the while blaming time constraints for his lack of curiosity and reluctance to embark again on personal development.

Fortunately, his willingness to consider his friend's passion and rational explanation helped him admit that the preponderance of waste in his work demanded way too much of his attention and that he might be willing to pay the price of change. Once he acknowledged the possibility of improvement, his desire for change ignited a willingness to learn. Wouldn't it be wonderful if all leaders experienced this transformation?

THE INTENSIVE

This intensive is carefully crafted to stimulate the group's journey toward becoming a functioning learning team.

Adult learning is enhanced through a host of stories, dialogues, surprises, humor, interactions, and relevant tasks that honor participant values, experience and education. We recognize that although no one person offers the complete answer, each adds value. And together, as adults, they can resolve thorny issues by engaging in ideological conflict.

The unique personalities, styles and perspectives of two facilitators contribute significantly to the learning experience. Both stay actively involved, but as one takes the lead, the other observes, supports and stores up a little energy.

These adult learning elements would enhance the success of most business meetings.

THE FOUR PILLARS

Everything in Part 1, The Collaborative, is based on four pillars: moments of truth, eliminating waste through Lean, mistake-proofing, and leadership bundles. These are the seminal concepts that must be used if we are to become true leaders. They support the leadership canopy that protects our customers, staff, products and selves from the vagaries of assumptions and inattention.

"Moments of truth" is a most important concept. Each choice we make, each behavior, perhaps each feeling, is a moment of truth that reveals our character, who we have become and how much further we need to go. Reaching any goal involves many moments of truth, opportunities for decision-making, any of which can be rationalized, minimized, delegated, or even ignored. Paying attention to the choice points and ensuring that each choice is optimal, based on the lofty standards of a clearly defined and communicated value system, gets us as close to true leadership as anyone can.

Jan Carlzon's book, *Moments of Truth*, superbly illuminates the moment of truth concept from a business perspective.

One of the best resources for taking a deeper look into leadership behaviors as a source of waste in most organizations are the writings of M. L. "Bob" Emiliani. Bob is the author of *Better Thinking, Better Results,* a Shingo Prize winner for its coverage of Wiremold's lean transformation and its emphasis on the importance of dealing effectively with people during a transformation.

Like Emiliani, we assert that the most productive breakthroughs that will occur next in business will come from eliminating behavioral waste. Most leaders don't pay much attention to the waste they create in their daily work, much of which customers and employees would not willingly pay for if given a choice. Leaders might ask, "How much value did I add today? How much waste did I create today?"

"Mistake-proofing" is all about paying attention, seeing and caring. When we *poka yoke* something, the poka yoked system makes the right thing happen regardless of how inattentive we are. But since not much is poka yoked, we must *self-check* to correct and *successive check* to correct in order to identify and rectify errors before they become defects that affect end-user customers.

"Leadership bundles" is also a most powerful concept. It focuses on "Have I done everything I should and nothing I shouldn't?" It battles relativism and uncertainty by proclaiming that bundled behaviors, when applied together, provide the very best evidence-based practice and assure us that other behaviors are unnecessary. It is a huge claim with evidence to support it.

We believe the bundles presented in this book are some of the most important. Leaders fail to use them for two primary reasons: first, they simply do not understand the value of applying leadership bundles. Their training in the technical aspects of running a business dulls their appreciation for the human factors needed to get the work done right. They seem to get away with this ignorance because the leadership bar is set so low that a smart, hard worker can reach the top with only primitive people skills. In an age where jobs-for-life are disappearing, people skills are becoming critical.

And second, people skills are hard to master. It isn't easy to stand between combatants and tell them a difficult truth. It isn't easy to admit, "I don't know" or "I was wrong." Just as Rudy followed procedures as his plane fell from the sky, a true leader steadfastly performs each element of a bundle to maximize the likelihood of success.

Much of our inspiration comes from the Kaizen concept of incremental and steady change. The term means to break apart and improve. Bundles allow you to break apart your leadership and improve individual components by applying evidence-based elements. As you become proficient with one bundle, you are likely to apply other bundles in a constant process of leadership improvement.

PONDERING

Most leaders we have queried bemoan their lack of time for anything but putting out fires. Responding to this concern, Rudy once coached a county executive to free up 30% of his work time so he could devote it to strategic planning, pondering the future. After a few months of coaching, the responsibilities of his department heads were adjusted, these department heads became a leadership team, and the executive got his 30%.

Having time to ponder does not necessarily guarantee positive outcomes, which are somewhat dependent on the quality of the pondering. Pondering is often a scattering of thought, less linear than topical. Unpracticed leaders may need to obtain some advice and practice on how to ponder.

The concepts of leader and follower offer a false distinction for true leaders. A true leader leads budding leaders. A nominal leader leads ignorant or trapped followers. We might also make a distinction between a true follower and a nominal follower. True followers always lead themselves as they make choices and apply the four pillars to following.

THE ZEN OF LEADERSHIP

First a mountain, then no mountain, then a mountain again. So many of us are myopic, blinded to the details, blinded to the entirety, blinded to this metaphor. Potential true leaders pay the price to experience the three phases of the mountain starting with seeing the mass which demands little rigor and offers only possibilities. Then, as in this collaborative, they rigorously focus on the detail and nuances of true leadership revealed in the four pillars. And then pursue their own quest for the mountain again. The mountain again, by the way, is the fulfillment of the greater-good potential within all of us.

Another way to benefit from this metaphor is to understand the first mountain is our own creation. We own the mountain and are responsible for its effects. When there is no mountain, we are focused on ourselves. It's like paying attention to buying the right hiking shoes before attempting to climb the mountain. Then, when the mountain appears again, it is everyone's mountain. At least, that's how we see it.

BUILDING TEAMS

A leader isn't a leader without followers, usually a group formed to accomplish a defined task in a set amount of time. True leaders create teams of followers who meet very specific criteria. Unlike nominal leaders, they do not simultaneously allow minimally functioning people to remain on the team and expect higher functioning team members to continue to be increasingly productive. We are convinced that Rudy's Four-Part Teaming Model is essential to quickly form and then maintain a high functioning team. It asks, does each team member:

1. Agree that the task is compelling, not trivial
2. Have a sense of membership, of belonging
3. Positively influence the team's decision-making
4. Receive sufficient personal rewards for participating?

We think that Lencioni's *The Five Dysfunctions of a Team* is his most useful teaming book. With any dysfunctional group, have everyone first complete the Lencioni fifteen-item survey. Then explain Lencioni's model and discuss what the scores mean. Most participants answer honestly and are usually motivated by "scores" in the "probably need to work on it" range. Take your time with this process. It is easy to reject ambivalent people or include those who don't belong.

A TEAM WITH A VISION

It is interesting that this team's vision statement, "unleash the power of leadership bundles" is similar to that of Star Trek, "Space, the final frontier." Both hold our gaze and draw us in. Neither explicitly declares, "We will lead; we will be the best; we will…" This collaborative team understood that mistake-proofing leadership will lead to their vision as certainly as, "To go where no one has gone before" leads to the immensity of space.

As Harriet said, most visions are flat, merely chains of clichés. We believe this is true because many leaders (1) do not understand what a vision does, (2) are not willing to engage in the visioning process long enough to evoke meaning, and (3) succumb to the least common denominator of people unwilling to invest in seeing.

Bob and Rudy once led a Change Mastery collaborative during which the learning team developed a vision of becoming change masters, "Our staff will beg for change—and want to make it happen."

HARNESSING THE SPEED OF THOUGHT

The nature of life is to identify and solve problems. Changes in our situation often mandate changes in what we do. Changes in our expectations do the same. The better we identify what the problem is and the clearer we are about what we want to accomplish, the easier it is to find a solution.

One of our change mastery students was featured in the Wall Street Journal for his innovative approach to aligning hospital clinics with corporate customers. He carries Harnessing the Speed of Thought with him on an index card. An administrative director, we'll call Jim, told us he approached our former student with a thorny problem that had resisted his every attempt to resolve. Our student pulled out his card and started with #1, "What's the issue?" Jim reported that "Within 5 minutes, I had the solution. He led me through it one step at a time."

Step one, the issue, is similar to using the "5 whys," a bedrock Lean practice used to identify root cause. Step 2, the goal, links to visioning. Step 3, the hurdles, links to logical and emotional concerns. Step 4, possible solutions, evokes both Kaizen improvement and innovation. And Step 5, the best solution, is the culmination of Lean, it's mistake-proofing mistake-proofing.

For those who say they don't have time for HST, we reply, "Until you find the time, you and yours will continue swirling in the waste of your own creation."

DELEGATING

This is a simple bundle. And yet, delegating is difficult for most leaders because (1) they don't understand how to do it well and (2) they mistakenly believe that doing the work themselves takes less time and produces better results. Stephen R. Covey in *The Seven Habits of Highly Effective People* clarifies how and when to delegate.

Young Zack said, "It was because I knew what to do." How did he know? Because his dad played the entire 5-step delegation out in his mind before approaching his son. He prepared and then behaved respectfully. That's what true leaders do. Nominal leaders, even if they do some pre-thinking, don't use the entire bundle.

Step 1, desired results, is all about the goal based on a significant issue: the issue is a garage so messy that the car won't fit; the goal is to get the car in and bring a little order. Step 2, guidelines, are the details about what to do. Step 3, resources, are what can be used to do it. Step 4, accountability, is about return and report—the time and place. And Step 5, consequences, is about what will happen as a result of success or failure.

CUSTOMER AND EMPLOYEE LOYALTY

The quest commonly known as customer satisfaction should really be customer loyalty. And staff satisfaction should be staff loyalty. Fred Lee asserts in his book, *If Disney Ran Your Hospital,* that customers who give fives on satisfaction surveys (using a one to five scale) are six times more likely to recommend a service to their family, friends and neighbors than those who give fours. Fives represent loyalty, fours only satisfaction. Loyal customers and staff receive more than they expect and therefore will stick with you through thick and thin, singing your praises to the masses. Loyalty, of course, is hard to come by.

We also like that Fred Reichheld's book, *The Ultimate Question,* teaches how to measure customer satisfaction and how to assure that your best customers determine the goods and services you provide.

Leonard Barry says in his book, *Discovering the Soul of Service,* that service is a promise. The more you promise and deliver, the greater the loyalty. Slip once and the loyal will stick with you while the only satisfied move on. Slip again and the relationship of trust may be lost and will be difficult to regain.

We believe the loyalty bundle composed of the Four-Cs (connect human-to-human, collaborate, contribute and confirm) and Development Dimensions International's Take the H.E.A.T. (hear them out, empathize, apologize, and take action) can contribute much to creating and maintaining customer and staff loyalty.

Connecting and collaborating lead to a partnership focused on clarifying customer issues and working toward customer goals. Contributing is the reason customers appear in the first place. And confirming answers the question, "Is this the best response for the customer and the company?"

Every step of Take the H.E.A.T is conceptually simple and behaviorally difficult. Hear them out seems very difficult until you treat them as a customer. It requires compassion toward someone who is irate, childish or even irrational. Empathize is also difficult as it requires you to identify the emotional content and name it in a way that softens, not inflames. Apologize seems the easiest, but we have found that many staff struggle with "Why am I apologizing? It's not my fault!" They exemplify Lencioni's Inattention to Results dysfunction; i.e., the focus on ego rather than team success. And take action is all about doing something that adds value.

INTRODUCING A CHANGE

The Four-Part Teaming Model sets the stage for presenting change by giving people reasons to participate. After clearly stating the proposed change and answering clarifying questions, the agenda applies David Cooperrider's Appreciative Inquiry, which gains its strength from (1) starting with positive views of the change, and (2) applying parallel thinking; i.e., having participants simultaneously focus their minds on an issue from the same perspective. Harnessing the Speed of Thought also employs parallel thinking by systematically focusing everyone sequentially on each of its five steps.

Appreciative inquiry begins with a positive view, which helps everyone acknowledge that there is good in the proposal; then the negative, their concerns and doubts; then what should be done, based on their values and the goodness of the proposal; and finally what people are willing to do, based on valid constraints while keeping standards high.

Edward de Bono's Six Thinking Hats, which we did not cover in this book, also uses parallel thinking. Participants metaphorically first put on a yellow hat and list all the positives about the issue. Next, the purple (formally black) hat to list the concerns or negative thoughts about the issue. Then the white hat, what more information is necessary and how it can be obtained. Fourth, the red hat, for feelings about the issue. Fifth, the green hat for participants to let loose their creativity about where this change might lead. Last is the blue hat which is worn by the facilitator or organizer who decides on the idea to be addressed and which hat to wear during the process.

ORGANIZATIONAL CHANGE

Bob's HST model for change is deceptively simple. It mandates involving people before change is even considered. For small groups (including families), to large corporations, if you want the smoothest and most effective path to change, let people know what problem or opportunity exists and let them walk every step along the way to implementing the response.

"Resistance to change" seems to be an accepted cost for change efforts when it doesn't have to exist at all. If people recognize that there is an issue that must be addressed, they will be anxious to address it. If you provide a solution to a problem they don't understand, of course they will resist. Mistake-proofing leadership is about getting and responding to feedback, not ordering people around. This is especially important and useful in change management at the beginning; we must agree we have a critical problem to address.

Another element of the HST Model for Change is the use of teams. Creating a team to address the change mandates finding a common goal and effort, the compelling task. It mandates everyone having a voice. It also mandates defining a positive outcome. A change announcement from on high is asking for, and usually results in, disaster.

Use the HST Model to mistake-proof your change efforts.

TIME

The wise use of time reveals a true leader. Whining about the perceived lack of time exposes the nominal leader, a victim who closes his or her mind, dismisses new ideas, and rejects opportunities to learn. "There isn't enough time," is the number one hurdle for leaders dealing with change, or so they say. For most, the real issue is priorities. We are amazed that so many so-called leaders allow the trivial to override the important.

Bob illuminates the issue this way. "If you had a terrible disease that required two hours of treatment every day for the next two years, would you find the time to get the treatment?" Yes, of course; treatment would be the priority. The difficulty for most is a reluctance to set aside old habits and venture into the unknown. They seem to prefer stress and whining more than chancing something new.

Stephen R Covey's self-management grid is conceptually simple. Everyone thinks they get it. Few, however, discover that liking the idea is not enough. Applying it makes the difference. And the most benefit comes from spending time in quadrant two. Vision, mutual goals, a focus on the compelling task and team results are all part of quadrant II.

COMMUNICATING

Although Andrew missed a collaborative session, our experience is that most participants do not miss any. Like Andrew, the few who miss do so because of illness or unavoidable demands.

There are three important take-a-ways about communicating effectively:

1. It is absolutely necessary to give and receive feedback, especially when the message is complicated or critical
2. Ensure successful communication by having the receiver repeat back the message
3. Tell stories, particularly of your own experiences, both good and bad, whenever possible.

LEARNING ORGANIZATIONS

Creating a learning organization is not easy. Nor is reading Senge's seminal work, *The Fifth Discipline*. We believe the key is to emphasize development *and* performance without one disrupting the other. True leaders can do this. Read his book and apply his principles. It will take a lifetime.

MISTAKE-PROOFING MISTAKE-PROOFING

This chapter shows the iterative nature of topics and conversations. It also reveals the importance of using Harnessing the Speed of Thought (HST). We believe that mistake-proofing mistake-proofing represents a viable bundle of the necessary and sufficient, evidence-based content leading to measurable results initiated by the vision and supported by andons to help us stay on track.

This chapter also declares the value of celebrating successes. We have tried many forms, but the most powerful have included sharing our contributions and rewards. When we skip this sharing, we always feel a loss of closeness and closure and a loss of self-respect for neglecting this important element.

ROSE

Rose, a true leader, demonstrates the essence of our work, mistake-proofing her leadership through the integration and application of leadership bundles.

It is beyond the scope of this book to explicitly provide bundles to mistake-proof every leadership activity. Our intent was to use examples of evidence-based bundles with which we are intimately familiar, particularly those that apply to situations typically fraught with waste. And to present our thinking in a manner that will help average human beings become true leaders.

The best approach is to study the bundles, inform others of your intent to use them, teach others the bundles, try them out, and welcome continuous feedback. Those who do this will become better leaders.

And most critical of all is to care; to care about people, processes, results and values almost in equal measure. Rose was a metaphor for all people. We added her to emphasize what is most important.

May you become the leader the world needs you to be.

INDEX

4-3-2-1 rule, 108
4-C's, 187
5 whys, 212

After enlightenment, 65
agenda for change, 130, 145
andons, 177
Appreciative Inquiry, 136

Barry, Leonard, 128, 214
Basic Agreement, 78
best practices, 3
Better Thinking, Better Results, 46, 205
blind basketball shooter, 195
Bryant, Bear, 69
bundles, 81, 82, 85, 176, 177, 192
business scandals, 42

Carlzon, Jan, 205
Carrie, Bob, 9
charismatic leader, 61
Churchill, Winston, 143
coaching, 193
collaborative, 5
communications bundle, 156
components of communication, 154
Cooperrider, David L., 136
Covey, Stephen, 111, 116, 149, 213
Covey's delegation model, 190
Covey's model, 114
creating a compelling vision, 92

DDI, 122
de Bono, Edward, 216
delegating, 114
delegation bundle, 110
Development Dimensions International, 122
Discovering the Soul of Service, 128
Donovan, 64

Effective leadership, 43
Eisenhower, Dwight D., 140
Emiliani, M. L. "Bob," 46, 47, 205
evidence-based medicine, 3
evidenced-based medical bundle, 55

feedback, 155
fifth discipline, 161
first there is a mountain, 64
Five Dysfunctions, 161
five principles, 49
five steps, 103
Flow, 49, 50
flying lesson, 38
follower, 34, 59, 60, 61, 208
four C's, 119, 128
Four-Part Teaming Model, 75, 77, 81, 95, 126, 129, 196

good idea, 60
greater good, 43, 44, 70, 71, 181

H.E.A.T, 122, 127, 129
Harnessing the Speed of Thought, 108, 126, 173, 196
Harnessing the Speed of Thought' bundle, 106

If Disney Ran Your Hospital, 214
influence others, 60

Kaizen, 207
Kotter, John, 145

Leadership, 42
Leadership bundles, 206
leadership team building bundle, 96
leadership value stream, 50
Lean thinking, 45
learning organization, 162
learning organization architecture, 160
Lee, Fred, 214
Lencioni, Patrick, 76, 95, 210
Lencioni model, 81, 84
Lincoln, Abraham, 70
loyalty, 118, 127, 128
loyalty bundle, 119, 127

measurement, 177
mental models, 159
mistake-proof leadership, 175
mistake-proof our mistake-proofing, 174
mistake-proof your leadership, 29
Mistake-proofing, 162
Mistake-Proofing bundle, 170
mistake-proofing leadership, 30
model, 192
Moments of Truth, 40, 205
moral compass, 43
Murphy's Law, 53
mutiny, 60, 61

no mountain, 67
nominal leader, 26, 43, 44
nominal leader characteristics, 20

Ob-Quest technique, 157
office manager, 67
Ohno, Taiichi, 46, 47, 69
Oshry, Barry,161

Perfection, 49, 52
personal mastery, 159, 160
perspective, 193
poka yoke, 4, 53, 54, 206
process check, 134
Pull, 49

quadrant two, 151

Reichheld, Fred, 214
resolve every conflict, 99
Rudy's model, 145

satisfaction surveys, 214
SBAR, 156
Scouting, 42
see-feel-change, 174
self-check, 53, 177, 184, 206
self-management grid, 219
Senge, Peter, 158
setting boundaries, 116
Seven Habits of Highly Effective People, 213
shared vision, 159
sharing, 222
Six Thinking Hats, 216
solve every problem, 99
speed of thought trap, 102
successive check, 4, 53, 54, 206
successive checks, 193
systems thinking, 159

Taiichi Ohno, 45
Take the Heat, 128
team learning, 159
The 7 Habits of Highly Effective People, 149
The Fifth Discipline, 158
The Five Dysfunctions of a Team, 76, 210

The Five-Dysfunctions of a Team, 96
The Heart of Change, 138
The mountain, 209
The Soul of Service, 214
The Toyota Way, 47
The Ultimate Question, 214
Thoreau, David, 148
Thumb Method, 83
time constraints, 148
tops, middles, bottoms, 161
Toyota Management System, 4
Toyota Production System, 45, 228
Troy, 166
true leader, 16, 45, 71, 207
Try it; learn from it, 11

University of St. Andrews, 167

Value, 49, 89
value stream, 49
Value Stream, 49
vision, 88, 175, 176
vision statements, 87

Wall Street Journal, 212
week's vacation together, 101
When should I lead, 62
working group, 89

Zack, 111

THE AUTHORS

Rudy F. Williams, Ph.D. was an educator, organization development consultant, and executive coach passionate about creating learning environments that help clients embrace change.

He enjoyed 35 years of practical experience and advanced education in an extensive array of theories, models, and interventions such as appreciative inquiry, systems thinking, accelerated learning, the Toyota Production System, leadership, open space and future search.

Some organizations in which he practiced include Arthur Anderson, Boeing Commercial Airplane Group, DuPont, U.S. Department of Labor, Olympic National Park, Simplot Company, Snohomish County, the United States Postal Service, and Virginia Mason Medical Center.

He earned an undergraduate degree in economics from the University of California, Berkeley; a masters in Organizational Behavior from Brigham Young University and a Doctorate in Organizational Behavior from Case Western Reserve University.

He held an airline transport pilot (ATP) rating and an instrument flight instructor (CFII) certificate and logged 8,000+

hours. As an avid backpacker, he thru-hiked the entire Pacific Crest National Scenic Trail from Mexico to Canada (2,651 miles) in the year 2000. He and his wife lived near Seattle and had four children.

Bob Brown, Ph.D., has been an independent performance enhancement coach for forty years. His expertise is helping individuals and groups to achieve their highest good.

Bob does mostly workshops (see www.collwisdom,.com) and the odd presentation and keynote address.

He lives with his wife Deena near Seattle.

His recent management books are:

The HST Model for Change
Enhancing the People Side of Organizational Development
A new approach to creating and sustaining change

Lean Thinking 4.0
Applying Lean tools and concepts to people interactions

New Darwinian Laws Every Business Should Know
(With Patrick Edmonds)
How to avoid making classic, fatal mistakes

The People Side of Lean Thinking
A Practical Guide to Change, Employee Engagement and Continuous Improvement
How to create a Lean friendly organization

Transparent Management
Unleash the Collective Genius of Your People
In depth look at Harnessing the Speed of Thought, the Four-Part Teaming Model, and other ideas

Earn Their Loyalty
Treating Customers and Employees Like People
A full presentation of the Four Cs and other concepts

Contact Bob at bob@collwisdom.com

Special Bonus
Chapter One from *The HST Model for Change*

BROKEN FLASHLIGHT

Organizational Development (OD) can be like changing a tire in a cold rain, in the dark, with a flashlight that only works if you shake it just right. Born about eighty years ago, OD is a dynamic field with roots in sociology, psychology, systems theory, organizational learning and a host of other approaches to help organizations adapt and develop.

For the short and so far meandering life of organizational development, there have been countless efforts to understand the people side of implementing change. Some have championed the concept that change is so odious that only by applying psychiatric type treatment for grief reactions can we overcome the trauma. Others promote applying the power of psychological tests to understand the complexities of people and thus enable customized interactions. Many focus on the rigidities of company culture while perhaps an equal number are split on declaring the effect of leaders as the major force to be blamed or to be hailed as the secret to success.

Fans of the complexity of change tout Everett Rogers' adoption process of knowledge, persuasion, decision, implementation and confirmation. The adoption of this process is often depicted in the labels attached to standard deviations on a bell curve: Innovators, Early Adopters, Early Majority, Late Majority and Laggards. These labels are taken as truth to the extent that naïve OD professionals believe that for every hundred people in an organization, thirty-four will comprise the late majority and should be helped in various ways. This weak thinking gives me a stomachache and OD a black eye. Categorizing people and then creating helpful interventions for these categories is an unnecessary and counterproductive complication to change efforts.

A possible title for this book could have been: *How Dumb Is OD Anyway?* Elisabeth Kübler-Ross and her portrayal of someone facing a terminal illness does not belong in the work setting and is not the classic response employees experience when facing change yet is widely promoted anyway. If you like this approach, especially the so-called change curve with the "pit of despair" at the bottom (often making an attractive PowerPoint slide), read Kübler-Ross' writings on her system, and you will know better. She said her model is not all-inclusive, that the order can and does change and, she emphasized, grief is an individualized experience. How such a wobbly platform could become an accepted OD model is beyond me.

Psychometrics also seems to be an OD magnet. The Myers-Briggs Type Indicator and similar vehicles for stuffing people into boxes is at best semi-science (and I believe another embarrassment for OD) and at worst a biased and prejudicial stereotyping of unique human beings. I am truly concerned about using methodology based on debunked psychoanalytic thinking or unsubstantiated theories. Using such tools is not how to make sense of change for the people involved. If you're doing that, please stop. Before you're tempted to use psychosocial instruments, check out validity and reliability studies done by neutral parties. I believe you will appreciate the folly of categorizing people. It is true such inventories make humans more understandable and seemingly available to targeted interventions, but so does stereotyping by race, religion and gender. Measures such as DISC and Personal Styles that identify simple behavioral tendencies can be useful if they celebrate and support differences and don't assume to plumb the intricacies of personality.

Using models as tools means we do not design interventions based on abstractions, such as personality types, but on actually occurring events—in our case, people interactions. It doesn't matter what kind of interaction or the differences of the people involved or the significance of the topic. What matters is how well the people involved can address the issue at hand. The HST model creates a process for effective people interactions. The model is used as a tool when it is useful and is discarded when it isn't. (The right tool makes an activity easier and more efficient.) People are free to choose what is best for them.

Currently, OD practitioners advocate using a four-step approach to improve organizations:

- Diagnosis
- Action planning
- Implementation
- Evaluation

With our model we have taken the first two steps for you and hope our efforts will stimulate you to take the last two using the HST change model.

Our *diagnosis* is that organizations do not understand change and have been misled about how to do it well. This conclusion is based on OD using suspect tools and models and on the limited success organizations seem to have when implementing change. Additionally, if we define company culture as the solidification of people interactions, we might wonder about de-solidifying interactions to create avenues for people and processes to change.

Our *plan* is to improve how employees understand change and shepherd that enhanced awareness through two critical elements of an organization. As we shall see, organizational development does not have to be traumatic. People are not incomprehensibly complicated. Learn just a couple of ideas and you can do what must be done without continually shaking that flashlight.

www.ingramcontent.com/pod-product-compliance
Lightning Source LLC
Chambersburg PA
CBHW071656090426
42738CB00009B/1553